Preface

This book is for all the people ~~caught up in these~~ issues and pulling their hair out, remember one day you will laugh about it.

This is not a HR manual or guide but a snapshot of real situations that have occurred with some thoughts and insights. You might laugh, you might cry but you might also be prepared if it happens to you.

This book was written during the COVID-19 pandemic during lockdown. Some of the stories may well prove to be an historical account of HR issues back in the times when most people went to the office for work but most of the issues are very current and often entail how tech in the workplace can cause HR headaches.

Thank you to all my friends and colleagues in Crystal Valley Tech (CVT), the cluster promoting Southeast Tech for their inputs. CVT is headquartered in Waterford, Ireland's oldest City. The southeast of Ireland is the biggest economic region outside the Capital Dublin, and is a region growing fast and growing smart.

No one is identifiable in this book, all details have been changed, locations, genders, outcomes etc. So, there is no need for anyone to panic!

"It's fine to celebrate success but it is more important to heed the lessons of failure".
Bill Gates, Co-founder of Microsoft

"Businesses face continuous change and evolution but the pace of change in leveraging digital transformation is momentous. It has never been more important that management support their people. HR is a critical function to help people adapt, grow and develop in these changing times".
Tom O'Keeffe, Head of Finance Business Partners - Growth at Glanbia Ingredients Ireland

"Speaking from a Micro business / Start-up point of view, as we grow staff in the new COVID -19 normal, HR managers' role is to ensure productive, effective and regular communications. Building trust and loyalty is critical as people become much more self-directed in their work without daily supervision. Sharing the wins both personal and professional with the team is critical, as balancing the feel-good factor with the pressure when the pressure is on knits people together".
Ann-Marie Mc Sorley, CEO and Founder of Veri

"HR is an often-neglected discipline within start-ups, ignore it at your peril, too many companies save a few Euro at the start of their journey, only for it to cost a multiple later".
Barry Downes, Managing Partner Sure Valley Ventures

"Your work is going to fill a large part of your life, and the only way to be truly satisfied is to do what you believe is great work. And the only way to do great work is to love what you do. If you haven't found it yet, keep looking. Don't settle. As with all matters of the heart, you'll know when you find it".
Steve Jobs, Co-founder Apple

"HR leaders should be empathetic, not sympathetic. I want my staff to be happy to talk with HR and never fear a HR meeting".
Sandra Whelan, COO and Co-founder of VR Education Holdings

"HR leaders of the future need high emotional intelligence and an interest in analytics… technology and people analytics because as the world changes, the way people interact changes too".
Crystal Valley Tech Co-founder

"HR managers of the future will need to have an understanding of an employee's ability to add value to the organisation rather than just do a job, they need to understand and grow with technology and they need to be able to manage remote working in a way that means productivity isn't compromised".
Ciaran Cullen Chief Navigator and Co-Founder at Handheld Technologies

"As digitalisation continues to drive the convergence of the work and home environment HR will be required to take a broader holistic approach to people development and to the organisation's contribution to a more sustainable society. Future HR education will balance traditional business with sociology and psychology".
Professor Willie Donnelly, President of WIT

"I believe the greatest asset any organisation has is its people. People deserve to be nurtured, supported and empowered to be at their best. This is a key differentiator of excellent HR, as a catalyst for burnout prevention and workplace vitality".
Dr. Mark Rowe, Medical Doctor, Author & Vitality Expert

Nude
Rude
Lewd
Crude
Screwed
& Sued

50 HR Stories from the Modern Workplace

Elaine Fennelly

Contents

INTRODUCTION

In March this year, 2020 the Covid-19 pandemic took hold and I had no more excuses, for years I had been threatening to write a book listing out all the ridiculous, funny, sad, crazy, dark, lewd stories from my work life across five multinationals, five start-ups in multiple sectors, IT, pharma, manufacturing etc.

I have also accumulated quite a few stories from the many CEOs, founders and HR leaders that I have interacted with daily over the last few years too.

As the pandemic played out, it became obvious within a short few months that the world of work would NEVER be the same again. Companies who had for years opposed working from home with every possible excuse managed to embrace this phenomenal change within weeks.

We are in the middle of huge change in society and the workplace, in my opinion will never be the same again. This sounds very scary and vague but people who worked before 1990 - 1995ish will remember a world of work without Windows or the Internet and most importantly without Mobile Phones.

Within a couple of years of their invention almost every desk and factory had a windows computer and internet access, this transformed so many roles and brought realtime information to people within seconds, for the first time ever.

I remember at the time people returning to work from career breaks and literally not recognising the world they were coming back to. Paper based processes had been replaced by computers within a couple of years.

I can also still recall navigating 8 lanes of traffic driving to New York for the first time from Washington using a map on my lap, no Sat Nav or google maps back then and that was only in 2003. That is almost impossible now to imagine.

People will manage their way through the changes that are on the horizon, companies will manage and HR People will have to help manage everyone through it. The lessons of the past show us that we will make our way through it and come out the other side. Right now, it looks like home working will be huge, coworking spaces will explode and maybe the traditional office blocks will be things of the past. In the news right now, Amazon is in talks with large mall owners in the US to turn retail space into Amazon fulfillment centres according to the Wall Street Journal. What an utter transformation. Think about it we all now buy online to the point that the traditional store is now no more than a warehouse to fulfil our orders!

In a decade or so, it will be fascinating to find out about the HR and People issues that will need to be resolved in the new world of work. I suspect many of the existing problems will still be around but who knows?

Most of my HR stories are from my career and from the careers of the CEOs and founders I meet every day from around the Country.

Most of my HR stories involve the use of technology, in some form or other so they are still very relevant right in the middle of this pandemic.

While most of my career has been in finance roles, I have been involved in start-ups from incorporation through to sale, worked as a General Manager of a Multinational and for the past couple of years been CEO of a not for profit called Crystal Valley Tech or CVT. CVT is a Cluster, a networking organisation for promoting the Tech Firms in the Southeast of Ireland. The importance of cluster organisations as key drivers for industrial change is a quite recent phenomenon.

This book is NOT a HR manual or a guide on how to tackle HR issues in your organisation, there are plenty of books and courses around to do that and plenty of highly qualified HR people to help you out. This is a collection of short stories with my thoughts and commentary. If you find it helpful, great. If you are new to the workforce, this may be quite a revelation.

Think about it, there is now a generation brought up on mobile phones, who have every second of their life documented digitally. A generation that with the touch of a button or a voice command get a pizza delivered, their shopping done, box sets to watch, sets their house alarm, reviews CCTV footage, gets music and arranges a hook up. To think that this does not spill over into the workplace would be naïve. It does and sometimes in a disastrous manner. The reason is simple, the work world that their parents and teachers prepare them for is generally from an era without smart phones and technology that does everything for them. Of course, many parents work in high tech workplaces, similarly a lot of teachers are very tech savvy but there is always a generational gap.

In years to come managers will also be cut from the same cloth as their younger employees and be able to relate better to staff as they will have been exposed to technologies throughout their lives too.

Before anyone is panicky and thinking their story is in here, no one is identifiable, and the stories cover the past decade from workplaces around the country and further afield. All identifiable details have been changed. Note for Fr. Ted fans – this is not my Golden Cleric Awards acceptance speech!

This book is aimed at:

- People returning to the workplace after a break
- Newcomers to the workplace
- Graduates taking up their first role
- People new to management
- Anyone who is nosey and wants an insight into HR / management issues.

As you are reading through these examples, spare a thought for the people who need to sort out the mess left by these situations. They take hours and hours to resolve. Even a simple he-said, she-said results in interviews, investigations, hours of documentation, witness statements and meeting independent observers. This can be an absolute nightmare. Managing people in my opinion is the hardest job of all as human beings are so complicated. Numbers and spreadsheets are far easier to deal with – they don't change their stories!

With employees these days far more likely to know their rights and not be afraid to pursue legal action, it is imperative that companies handle all people issues carefully and stay on the right side of the law.

Remember too that many companies do not have a dedicated HR person so what happens is that managers with no HR experience or legal awareness try to sort out the most complicated issues. Start-up companies can be very guilty of cutting costs in the early days and not having a HR person, they leave the role of HR to

- The woman on the team if there is one.
- Finance - who often manage HR as its deemed administrative rather than technical
- Anyone who wants it or has time to deal with it.
-

Even in the most sophisticated companies that do have plenty of HR bodies on the ground it can often be incredibly challenging to resolve complex issues. Of course, it can be extremely rewarding to have and keep a happy workforce, but one issue handled badly can undue many years of good work. Confidence in a person or a company once damaged is hard to restore. Also, historical HR issues arise but the manager who was there at the time may have left the company or poor records may have been kept at the time or may even have been lost. Nightmare!

The good news is that there is an array of HR software out there now and many are modular so you can start quite inexpensively with basic staff contracts, add in staff handbooks, time and attendance systems, holidays, performance reviews etc. The list is endless and it is often difficult in the early days to know what path your company will take, so it is hard to choose the best software fit for your company. For that reason, so much of HR is manual, spreadsheets, emails, word docs, excel docs and notebooks.

My advice would be at the very least to set up a Dropbox or a secure document repository where at least all the documents relating to staff are kept together. Sounds basic but you would be amazed when it comes to company audits, sales, mergers, acquisitions how many key documents cannot be located. If you are selling the company, this could put a rather large dent in the price.

Wherever you do - store HR records properly and securely, don't put them on a computer drive that can be found by bored employees on a night shift looking in places where they shouldn't and then challenging their manager about the content.... sounds like time to jump into some story telling!

At the end of some of these stories you may decide that HR is the future for you and you relish the thought of sorting out all these issues or you may thank your lucky stars that you are an engineer, chemist, payroll clerk etc.

It is important to remember though that most employees are completely brilliant, they come into work, do a great job, are vested in the company's future and work hand in hand with management. Many of the mistakes they stumble into are not premeditated or malicious, it can simply be naivety or stupidity or both! Young people are incredible to work with, they bring energy, innovation and ideas every day to the workplace, they embrace change and stay incredibly enthusiastic despite living and working in very uncertain times. Every generation think they have it the toughest but without doubt graduates and school leavers today can not expect job certainty, secure incomes, a pension or in many cases afford to buy their own homes. That is truly tough.

Similarly, it is important to mention that most of the HR stories entail employees doing something wrong whereas in reality many leaders and founders are the ones who screw up. As Oscar Wilde said,

"Experience is simply the name we give our mistakes"

So enjoy the HR stories I have written and I have genuinely tried to put some learnings around them so that if you do encounter something similar you might know what to do or what not to do. It can be a very lonely journey when you are a HR lead or a CEO. There is often no one you can trust and if you do confide in someone you can run the risk that they are just waiting in the wings to exploit the information you might share with them. When I gave this book to a few close friends before publishing, many of them said it was a real relief to know that other managers had these issues to deal with and that sometimes they felt it was just them that had endless hours tied up in HR issues.

CHAPTER ONE
Soap Star

In case you have not realised it – everyone is taking selfies, many are taking nude pics, dick pics, whatever you want to call them. This is all very well until you follow through on what can happen, and what did happen. Meet Jason our new hire, he is in his company less than six months after graduating with a computer science degree and this is his first ever job. Jason and his girlfriend had a great 2 weeks in the sun, so great that Jason took over 150 pictures of his girlfriend in the shower in various poses and let's just say, she dropped the soap a lot and was very thorough with her soaping.

What Jason was deciding to do with his pics on his return to Ireland, who knows and who cares, who are we to judge?

However,

Jason comes back to work and is happy relaxed and suntanned, he is having a great day and notices that his phone battery is low so he does what every naïve graduate might do, he plugs his phone into his laptop to charge. Big mistake, why, because his phone then automatically transfers all his camera roll to the company laptop. Jason is no fool though and despite having a near cardiac arrest he attempts to delete the pics. But wait, Jason's company have forbidden and prevented deletion of all files on company property. He sits and sweats and realises he has two choices, say nothing or fess up.

He does the honourable thing and arranges to meet his manager. He then must tell Susan his manager that he has been very devious and attempted to delete files. Susan already knows this – the company software has alerted her that Jason had attempted to delete files, however upon reviewing said files with the company IT security officer, Susan has reason to believe that the girlfriend, let's call her "the Soap Star" is underage. Jason is a graduate and is 19 but his girlfriend is younger.

Susan now has a problem – should she ring the Police or should she just give Jason a warning? What if she does not ring the Police and it comes to light that the Soap Star is a minor? Susan also knows Jason's parents very well and that is how he got an interview for the job. Should she tip them off? How embarrassing for everyone concerned. What if Jason's Dad, a very volatile individual is furious with her? Yikes, Houston we have a problem.

So, what did happen to poor Jason? Well it transpires that the soap star was not a minor, luckily for both of them. Susan and HR had a frank chat with Jason and reminded him of the company policies. He then had a very long, toe curling meeting with the company security officer to review each image and delete them one by one.

Let us just say, it was a holiday Jason will not forget, nor will most of the management team who had to view his pics.

Now, the horror of this is minor compared to a company I spoke to, who had to contact the Police, as the pics they found on the company laptop were of nude children. These were harmless photos the parents took of their toddlers as keepsakes in their paddling pool on the veranda of their balcony. However, nude pics of young children on a company laptop was a serious case for concern and HR had no hesitation about getting the Police involved who had to interview the mortified mother. It took several days to resolve and caused stress all around. The laptop could not be used and luckily for the camera happy mother, the company were happy to issue an informal warning only.

I could fill an entire book on story after story of personal pics ending up on work servers, nude pics, pics of staff taking drugs, pics of ex-girlfriends, ex-boyfriends, pics of employees in compromising positions with their managers; the list is endless.

Some stories were also very sinister including a very sad case of a drunk girl with a group of men at the office Xmas party in a nightclub bathroom. Pictures were taken and somehow the pictures got introduced to work by mistake and then all of a sudden, the company is involved in a police investigation.

Think of your average day. How many people do you see on phones and taking pictures? You would be very naïve to think that some of them do not go astray.

Many schools now have visits from the Police who deliver very frightening, eye opening training on the abuse of mobile phone photographs. They detail cases of young men and young women encouraging people online to send on nude pics and then to find out that it is a much older person who will attempt to blackmail them for the return of the photographs. The Police don't hold back talking about suicides that have resulted from online mistakes that teenagers have made. As part of Crystal Valley Tech's promotion of tech, we go around to schools and meet guidance counsellors. They often encourage us to be open with the students and help them understand the consequences of technology. They often share harrowing stories of blackmail and sextortion within their schools and the cases are involving younger and younger kids all the time.

This kind of intervention from the police is brilliant, it is a very early induction program for teenagers into the world of work as it starts to get them to think about the consequences of using and abusing mobile phones.

Lessons learned

- The message is clear, mobiles are fabulous but be careful where you charge them. Do not charge them from your laptop or desktop at work. Do your charging at home and not in the workplace. Mobile phone theft is a massive business so it is best not to leave your phone unattended.
- Read your company policies carefully. Managers make sure you get your staff educated on your company rules. Taking extra time with new hires and graduates is so worthwhile as it could save your company so much time down the road and prevent so many issues from arising in the first place. A lot of induction programs now are very detailed about the use of phones and PCs.
- Every time you pose for a photograph, stop and think do I really want HR, IT, the Police etc. looking at it. This might make you put the camera away!
- Get legal advice immediately if you are dealing with minors. Do not hesitate, make sure you do not leave yourself open to any accusations. If you do involve the Police, they are brilliant and are very professional. This won't be their "first rodeo" and they will help you sort out the situation.
- If you are selling your company or merging it, you will have to declare all legal claims against your company which may cause the buyer to back off or drop the price if they see something they don't like, something that might cause an ugly headline down the road, so make sure you keep the claims away.
- I literally see no reason to video yourself or anyone else in the shower but if you do and you drop your soap, be careful of the camera angle when you pick it up. I kid you not :)
- I am not sure if Jason ever told his girlfriend but she got some strange looks that year at the Xmas party.

CHAPTER TWO
Branding Errors

It is late at night and Charlotte is on the help desk alone, bored and watching the clock. Her phone pings, brilliant it is the latest hook up she has met on a dating app.

After an hour of text exchanges and relief that she has had only one support call, she decides to send on a rude snap of herself. Harmless enough, she takes a cleavage shot. However, young Charlotte's preferred pic managed to include the company logo on the wall in the distance. Despite probably spending ages getting the right light, the right angle, she manages to miss a massive six-foot company logo.

Whilst the company in question provides support to customers, they do not sell lingerie. Charlotte was quite clever though; she did not show her head in the pic which made it even more difficult to track down when the pic made its way to Facebook and her team leader became aware of it. Eventually she was identified as the photo was time and date stamped and she was alone at work.

Charlotte did not fare very well at the ensuing disciplinary meeting; she had breached company policy by using her mobile at work. Her social media content was her own business apparently, but she was on probation and she lost her job immediately for Gross Misconduct.

Many companies love to brand their people with logos and company names on hoodies, hats, umbrellas, shoes, bags and pens. This has led to so many HR issues with the prevalence of Facebook and Twitter. Managers have arrived on Monday mornings to be faced with emails, complaints, calls from the Police tracking people down. Why? The list of footage that may have emerged is shocking. Footage with people wearing your logoed hoody engaging in animal cruelty, assaults on people, urinating on premises (right in front of the camera), vomiting, striking lewd poses on statues and landmarks and believe it or not shoplifting and thefts.

Lessons learned

- Know your company policies so you don't get sacked for doing something stupid.
- Stay off the dating apps in work no matter how bored you are.
- Managers of people should be very realistic about the use of mobiles. If workers are working shift work or late hours, they may well need to check in on children, spouses etc. Banning the use of phones is totally unrealistic and really aggravates staff. It is far more realistic to allow staff to spend a small amount of time on them, that way you build more trust.
- Needless to say, if mobile phones are a safety hazard stick to your guns on banning their use.
- Some of the companies I visit do not allow staff to use phones in the canteen areas as they are considered antisocial and staff seem to accept this. It encourages more chat and fun during the breaks at work too.
- Never underestimate what the public will report to management from what they see on social media, I am always amazed at the time people have on their hands to track down things that offend them.
- If buying branded merchandise which can be extremely expensive, have a thought to its use and how it might end up in the wrong place. Some companies only buy pens, keyrings etc. because they have been in the situation described above.
- If you are going to filter and photoshop your assets, make sure you photoshop the company assets too.

CHAPTER THREE
Nocturnal Activities

Nowadays, most jobs have computer input in some shape or form, from factory floor, to warehouse to office - most staff must use computers. In one large firm in Dublin there was a single PC for every four employees, and they shared the same login details – rookie error on behalf of the IT department.

What happened in this case was the PC was used for surfing hard core porn during the night shift. Never a good idea on a work PC and never a good idea if your IT department circulate reports highlighting such nocturnal activities.

What happened in this case was incredibly sad. The employee in question's wife worked in the company in a senior position at the time of this incident. The employee in question was undoubtedly the culprit as he was the only one on the team inputting data. However, he got a legal representative who argued that if there was a shared login and no CCTV, it was impossible to pinpoint the crime on him. Furthermore, the login details were kept on a piece of paper stuck to the screen. He kept his job and his entire team was sent to porn counselling classes. His mortified wife did not last awfully long in the company. Interestingly her husband did.

Lessons learned

- Never share a login with anyone. Never give your passwords to anyone. Never write your password on a post it and stick it to the PC. I am always amazed at what I see even in the most high-tech environments.

- Even the most rudimentary use of computers warrants proper policies and training. This protects both the employee and the employer. Review and update policies regularly, even if you are a start-up. Find the money for an IT consultant to do this if you do not have the skills in house. Most software vendors will provide extensive training, so stretch your budget as far as it will go. Document your training and do refresher courses regularly. Never be in the position where an employee is saying that they did not know they were doing wrong.
- Never underestimate people's abilities to misuse company computers. Some bored employees will find files they should not, look at material they should not and if they manage to do this you only have yourself to blame.
- Recognise that the workplace is totally different during the day versus during the night. Many offices are operating 24 x 7 hours to work on support and security. As a result, issues are becoming far more prevalent from night-time activities.
- Have a good legal defence if you want to keep your job. Seriously, never underestimate the advice you can get if you pay for it from an experienced professional.
- One of the biggest HR lessons I learned was that a 24 x 7 business is not the same as 9-5. This sounds obvious but far too many managers jump in without realising it is a different ball game. What happens in the early hours of the morning will never mirror what happens in the afternoon with management around. It is so difficult to set the culture and expectations of people when they spend very little time interacting with more senior staff. Always treat a move to 24 x 7 as seriously as a move into a different country or time zone. Recognise that you will have very little face time with your staff and you need to make it your business to call in from time to time at unsociable hours, even if it is just to say a passing hello.

CHAPTER FOUR
No Good Deed Goes Unpunished

Despite the low prices of PCs and tablets, most people who bring laptops home will use them for surfing the internet unrelated to work. Who can resist checking the weather, looking at the news or generally killing a few minutes looking at your favourite sites, sport, fashion or food?

Gillian was guilty of this crime; she was a diligent worker and regularly worked into the small hours communicating with the foreign head office.

One night her stressed out husband asked her to print of his college thesis at work the following day as his printer was dead. No problem she thought. Gillian tried to get the document via email but the file was massive. No problem she thought again as hubby gave her a memory stick and she loaded the files onto her laptop for a sneaky print off at 7am the next morning.

However, the next morning she discovered she had managed to put a corrupt file on the company server, one that could have caused unspeakable damage. Thankfully, her company had a good firewall and the file was caught, but her decision making was questioned by her new department manager.

Gillian was working for an IT company and should have known a lot better; she had also recently been promoted and was managing staff for the first time. Additionally, she had just completed 3 days of in-house training around compliance and company policy, the irony was not lost on her. Gillian confided that this single incident was the nail in the coffin of her career with this company. Gillian was also haunted by the fact that she could have caused a major security breach that might have ended the company's very existence.

Routinely parents are found printing their kid's school and college projects in work. Other examples include staff working on table plans for weddings and printing them off. People involved in GAA and other extracurricular activities often print off committee business in the office. This all comes at a huge risk - introducing files from external sources runs the risk of bringing a virus into the workplace and causing havoc.

I have heard story after story of factory downtime after staff had infected computer systems. If you work for a payments company, a bank or a company that manages sensitive information, your company may not survive if a breach of security occurs and the company is hacked. Think about that the next time you are tempted to print off your hotel booking confirmation. Thankfully, mobile phones are reducing the need to print off as much material as in the past.

Lessons learned

- Think, think think before you mix business and personal files.
- Read Hillary Clinton's "What happened" for more information on the consequences of mixing work and personal emails.
- Buy a home printer - they are cheap, attractive looking and very handy.
- Know that if you do introduce a virus to the company server, it will be traced to you in next to know time, so never try denying it, fess up and take your beating.
- If you see gaps in the company's security systems, highlight it to the IT folks. In recent years, I have been really surprised by breaches in security only for an employee to claim they knew it was a risk!

CHAPTER FIVE
Moxie Moron

Kevin was furious, he was a software engineer and had a crazy day ahead of him and his mac died. It just gave up at 11am in the morning. The deadline was four pm, but he was a crafty developer, everything was backed up to the company server in real time so all he needed was another mac and he could login. So of course, Kevin borrowed one of the company spare macs and very shortly afterwards found HR files including employee contracts detailing salaries. He read them, he noted them and he then used them in a conversation with HR. He simultaneously pointed out their lack of professionalism for leaving the files on a spare laptop and also pointed out his lower salary compared to his colleagues with similar qualifications and experience.

What did HR do?

They had to take it on the chin regarding the files but they also pointed out that he read files that he shouldn't have, pointing out it was the equivalent of finding a hard copy folder marked confidential and reading it regardless. It said a lot about Kevin's character too that he would do that.

But and it's a big but - what about his salary? He threatened to leave if he didn't get a pay increase as he was crucial to the delivery of a project. Guess what? He got his pay increase and a warning to stay quiet. The HR manager who did this told me that they knew they were doing wrong giving into him but the risk of him leaving was so huge and so crucial to securing new business that they sucked it up. If it was a larger company with more secure cash and sales Kevin might have been told to walk. Some of you may think Kevin very mean, some of you may admire his moxie!

- Wipe your spare computers and ensure your company has a proper procedure for managing spare laptops.
- Sometimes managers and team leaders at all levels compromise principles for the survival of the business, remember start-ups, scaling and large businesses are different beasts and require different skills.
- Understand that the skills needed to manage a big company are quite different to a medium or small one. Management skills although transferable are different in various sectors and sizes. Many managers fail fast when they do not understand this.
- Blackmailing for pay increases is not that unusual.
- Employees often claim they will leave if they do not get the increase they want. If you give in, they might shout their mouth off and start a precedent. If you don't give in, they may leave. Managers do what they need to do but all of them say the same thing - if someone starts down the road of threatening to leave, they will eventually leave, so recognise that and do what you need to do in the period they remain.
- If staff are routinely threatening to leave maybe, it's time to look at your pay rates and pay review process. If you have not got time to do this there are plenty of HR professionals that you can subcontract the work out to, often this approach can remove any bias you may have too.
- If you are faced with HR issues, feel out of your depth and do not have a dedicated HR person, join employers' organisations such as IBEC or ISME and for a relatively low price you can have great advice a phone call away.

CHAPTER SIX
Location, Location, Location

Lionel was an extremely successful project manager in a software company. He was also constantly looking for pay increases which the start-up company simply could not deliver on. However, the company won an extremely lucrative UK contract which ideally needed a person in the UK to deliver. Lionel volunteered to relocate to live in London for 12 months if he got a fifty percent pay increase. Reluctantly he got his pay increase. He was also a contractor and not a company employee and he spent very little time in the main office so was not missed too much. As it happened the company CEO needed to travel to London monthly for a meeting with this particular customer and would meet Lionel the day before. They typically spent at least a half day catching up in person and the following morning Lionel would attend the customer meeting with the CEO.

Park that thought for a moment. Now we meet the marketing lead of this company who decided to take a day off and go to IKEA Dublin. While having coffee in the restaurant there she saw Lionel on his laptop working away. Yes, you guessed it. To secure his pay increase Lionel pretended to move to London. He would fly over monthly to meet the CEO there and they would meet in a coffee shop or hotel near where he allegedly lived, claiming his flat was too small to accommodate meeting the CEO there. The UK Customer was a huge organisation, so Lionel used to ensure he was seen there once a month and it never dawned on anyone that he was not around for weeks on end. Also, Lionel was very clever and, on the company, social channel he would post photos weekly from various places in the UK, so he obviously took photos in advance to share around. These photos showed how much he was loving living in the UK.

- Clean up your social media or be prepared for it to impact your employment prospects. I recall at the time of the 2018 rugby rape trial, an individual who posted multiple comments about the girl who took the case which were judgemental and quite disgusting comments. These comments were seen by the hiring manager in the company he was interviewing with during a routine search of Facebook and needless to say he did not get the job. A lucky escape for that manager as the incident gave an incredible insight into the sick twisted mind of the job hunter.

- Check out the wayback machine or other similar websites that allow you to recover what you thought were deleted webpages. Yikes!

- Remember you can somewhat clean up your own social media channels, but you cannot clean up someone else's, so if your friends are taking pictures of you at a party, they could literally end up anywhere and impact your future.

- Also, what people put up on their social media channels is indeed their own business, you cannot fire someone because they posted something that you did not like. Obviously if they bring the company into disrepute or do something defamatory that is a different story. Also, no company can realistically monitor all their staff's posts no matter how hard they try but you can of course have software that notifies you of any mentions of your company name. That way at least you can ensure your company mentions are appropriate and legal.

- It is always unfortunate when you have to search a name which is the same as a thief, a murderer or a porn star. In the latter case, you then have HR reported to themselves for viewing porn star bios while at work, thinking they were looking at candidates they were about to interview.

CHAPTER EIGHT
Holy Joes

Lisa and Joe were having lunch at work when Lisa's sister rang her from New York to say she had just got engaged to her long-term girlfriend and that they would be getting married in a matter of weeks. An excited Lisa shared her good news with Joe. Joe was disgusted at the thought of two women getting married and said it was wrong and it was against his religion. The two got into a very heated ugly argument that ended up in Janet's office, who was the project manager that they both reported to. Lisa felt outraged that her colleague was so narrow minded, and Joe felt that he had religious beliefs that he was entitled to voice in the office.

Janet was struggling to know what to do, rather than ring a local employers' organisation to get Irish relevant advice she rang the US parent company who looked after HR. This was a big mistake. The advice from head office was to meet with the two employees and point out that discussions about religion, politics and such matters were best kept out of the office.

Employment legislation in Ireland means that you cannot treat people differently based on their sexual orientation, you cannot say that you do not like or approve of people based on their skin colour or their sexual orientation and indeed a list of other reasons. So, Janet did not handle that HR issue correctly. She should have ensured that the company handbook was clear about bullying and harassment in the workplace and she should have spoken to the employee in breach of it. All employees are entitled to be treated with dignity and respect in the workplace. Think about it, a company can be sued for not hiring a candidate if the reason was related to their sexuality – so why should discrimination be allowed from candidates on the payroll?

Other issues can arise in the workplace when people get into heated debates over day to day issues. It is hard for some younger hires in particular to navigate office politics. Nowadays, when twitter and social media are so polarised and people do not hold back giving their opinions, it is very difficult for some people to understand how to behave in the work environment. They need to understand that there is a code of conduct and that there is legislation protecting employees. You may believe same sex marriage is wrong but you cannot voice that in the workplace.

These issues can become more pronounced the more diverse the workforce becomes. Managers need to ensure their staff are respectful of people's backgrounds, religion and sexual orientation. They might privately be opposed but there is no place for voicing that at work.

In recent times US politics is becoming an extremely hot button in Irish workplaces. No matter what you think of Presidential Candidates and Presidents, do not voice it to your American Colleagues. It is fair to say that they take politics far more personally than we do in Ireland and it is a far more polarising subject.

Recognise that it is difficult for younger staff to adjust to the workplace, they are coming from an age when it is absolutely ok to put your views on social media. They see that many people do not hold back regardless of who they offend. Think about it, they get phones at 12ish and join you at 22ish, so they have social media feeds for a decade before they join a company. If this is their first real job, they may not be aware of the expectations of them in the workplace. It is your job to have a great induction plan and to live and role model a great inclusive culture.

- Make sure you have a good company handbook, rules on behaviour and a code of conduct for the office.
- Managers of people need to role model the behaviours expected of their reports, you cannot be a manager and be openly homophobic and then expect your staff to behave differently.
- Work on your culture, in my role in charge of HR in a multinational we had company lunches once a month where staff would do a presentation on their hobbies. The idea was to educate, to get to know the person a little bit better and to encourage fun and banter in the office.
- CEOs might often come from a technical background but if they are an Irish Director, they need to understand that they have obligations in a company which include upholding employment legislation. There are loads of supports out there if you can't afford a full time HR person, use the brilliant ISME or IBEC, both amazing employers' organisations. In the example above, the CEO could have simply placed a local phone call rather than assumed the US head office would know how to handle it.
- For the record there are many amazing HR staff working in US and overseas multinationals but there are many who haven't a clue!

CHAPTER NINE
On the Record

In the modern workplace, the annual review is now supplemented with weekly or monthly one on one chats with your manager, 360-degree feedback from your peers, customers, suppliers, managers etc.

Be prepared to be recorded if you are managing people. I cannot believe how many stories I have heard from CEOs and HR leaders about them being recorded without their permission even when it violates company policy.

To make matters worse, the Workplace Relations Commission (Irish Employment Legislation body) sometimes allow recorded evidence at their hearings even if it was done without permission. You would think with GDPR and privacy laws that people would be reluctant to record their boss or HR leader. Think again. This whole area is a minefield. You might be tempted to think – so what! I am not doing anything wrong but think again, what if the recording is edited selectively, maliciously put online, used as blackmail or circulated as a joke around the company etc. There are so many software packages out there now that you can edit any conversation with very little skill, I have seen demos of this by legal personnel and it is very scary to say the least. Also, the laziest, work-phobic people seem to have incredible skills when it comes to using technology to try and extract money from corporations.

Many of the CEOs I have spoken to say that they will only have performance reviews or meetings of any sort with a HR witness present. Many CEOs also tell me they will only meet once mobiles are left outside the meeting room, but you still don't know if there is a second mobile or recording device in the employees' pocket or elsewhere!

- If you are in business or going into business, know how you want to deal with recordings and expect to be dealing with issues relating to this matter.
- Legislation in this area is a moving target so get advice, every time. Do not assume you know the legal position as it may have changed since you last checked.
- Always assume going into a disciplinary meeting that you are being recorded.

The Irish Times reported in November 2019 that an employee in Northern Ireland won an unfair dismissal case but her award was reduced by 30 per cent, 10 per cent of which was attributed to the covert recording of her employer during a HR disciplinary meeting.

The employer appealed the decision but lost, one of the reasons being that the covert recording of her employer was not set out as an offence in the employer's disciplinary procedure either before or after her dismissal from the company. The employer felt it was inappropriate to be recorded without agreeing to it in advance.

CHAPTER TEN
Lush Life

It was late on a Thursday night and the contact centre staff had a major problem with their phone network, the supervisor Richard had left several hours earlier and was called back in. It became apparent that Richard was under the influence of some substance as his speech was slurred, his eyes were glassy and he was unable to fix the problem. Richard logged a call with the US head office and left. The next day one of the team members Rory who had witnessed Richard's behaviour reported him to HR.

Colin the HR leader was concerned. He had never witnessed Richard being anything but professional and he also knew that Rory and Richard had a history - both inside and outside work going back to a girl they both dated in the past. Colin thought long and hard about what to do. If he spoke and accused Richard, he knew Richard would deny the charges and Rory could face a backlash. So, he decided to do a random drug test on Richard which was entirely permissible and documented in the company handbook. Richard was shocked, gave every excuse and refused the drug test, he also chose to leave the company.

In many stories like this one the HR person has chosen to ignore the problem and in most cases it did not go away. In many workplaces drug taking is a gross misconduct offence meaning instant dismissal especially if the person is working with machinery.

This has proved tricky for companies as often a person with a positive drug test will apologise and beg for a second chance. If HR and management agree to that, they might be in breach of their own company rules. Also, an employer could lose an unfair dismissal claim if it is deemed the drugs / alcohol was a health issue and they didn't try to help the employee!

The drug stories told to me are endless, cases of drugs being found hidden in lockers, bathrooms, the canteen, cases of staff members seeing their managers taking drugs on staff nights out and being terrified of the backlash if reported. All good managers of people will have a zero tolerance towards drugs in their workplace. Drugs will by and large impede decision making and pose safety risks. Good leaders will tackle the problem i.e. get help or get them out. Poor leaders will accept working with drug users and do nothing about it. I recall a senior manager taking drugs at a Xmas party, I only found out about it after he had left the company when one of his direct reports told me. He had been too scared to say anything as he had just joined the company after a long period of unemployment. I felt terrible that it had happened, and that the junior employee didn't come to me. The manager taking the drugs in question could have jeopardised all our jobs and the junior person was willing to stand by and let this happen. When I asked him why he didn't tell me, he said that he didn't want to rat on his manager. I was shocked at the immaturity of this answer from someone almost middle aged. It made me incorporate some values training and whistleblowing training into the induction process.

Alcohol is a big offender too, I have heard of workers on night shifts drinking alcohol at work, groups drinking in the office an hour before they finish up for a staff night out. As with drugs, this is a simply unacceptable and most good companies have a zero-tolerance policy.

Lessons learned

- Have great company policies to guide you.

- I have always been a great believer of having a drugs test as part of the hiring process. This has not always gone down to well with some of my colleagues as drugs are increasingly used at weekends and as part of a night out by many people. Some Managers take them and so obviously object if you bring in a drugs testing policy. Some managers think casual drug taking goes hand in hand with creativity and that you are being too much of a "Holy Joe" if you do drugs testing. However, my personal opinion is that they cause too much trouble in the workplace. I have had to manage the fallout too many times from users and it impacts the individual, their colleagues and ultimately the company. A simple urine test as part of a medical will test for the most common drugs but if you are hiring someone who uses drugs, chances are they won't do the medical when they hear about the drugs test in advance. Win, win, you don't pay for their medical or hire a user.
- If someone has an alcohol / drugs problem and you have a medical program to help them out that is great. Many people have managed to turn their lives around and credit their employers for helping them.
- Remember if you provide alcohol at an event and your staff member comes into harm, you could be held liable. For this reason, many employers limit the alcohol provided or increasingly are not providing any alcohol.
- If someone arrives in work and smells of alcohol, tackle it immediately, talk to the person, send them home on pay if you have to but never allow them to continue working if you suspect they are under the influence. Better safe than sorry.
- Get expert help if you find yourself in this situation, it is a really tricky area to deal with a person with a drugs / drink problem and you could implicate the company in a legal case if you act too quickly without thinking of the consequences down the road.

CHAPTER ELEVEN
Party Party

The Xmas party has a bad name and deservedly so!

One such Xmas party happened a few years ago. A relatively large group went out to dinner without their project manager, who was on leave. The group stayed out, got progressively drunker and somewhere around 3am one of the males in the group Ben tried to kiss one of the girls Laura. He claimed it was a joke and they both laughed it off.

The following Monday however Laura went to her manager, crying and upset and told him the entire story, however she refused to make a formal complaint. This left the HR Leader, Jeff in an uncomfortable position; it would not be fair to Ben to sack him or reprimand him without giving him the right to reply. So Jeff called the Xmas party group together and told them that some stories had been leaked out about the night out and reminded them that they should realise they represent the company when they go out and that they should behave in a proper manner etc.

30 minutes later, Trevor, who was at the night out asked to chat with Jeff. He told Jeff that Laura had been outrageously flirting with Ben all night and had left the party and spent the night with him. Laura had massive regrets the next day apparently as Ben, despite being a sleazebag was married. Laura was spreading stories around the office about Ben, which was not unusual for her according to Trevor. Trevor was older and was wise to Laura's way and saw that she had destroyed Ben's reputation with senior management to further her own and he felt obliged to inform management. Time would prove he was correct and Laura turned out to be a very manipulative and devious individual.

What a mess! Jeff as HR manager was under serious pressure that week to get a new performance appraisal document over to head office in the US and instead had lost nearly 2 days' work with stories, fall out, getting advice and planning what to do. Nothing takes up more time than HR issues. They drag on, other people often get pulled into it, these conversations need to be documented meticulously to be fair to all involved. In the end Jeff did nothing further except speak to the CEO, explain what had happened and agree to no more nights out that involved alcohol.

I have heard stories of bars and hotels being damaged by staff, employees being involved in fist fights, staff drink driving after the event. The list is endless, so approach parties and nights out with caution and never assume work night out bad behaviour is limited to the younger members of staff.

Lessons learned

- Xmas parties are a red flag, as is any night out with large amounts of alcohol, so advise your staff in advance of the conduct expected.
- In this example, the girl who said she was assaulted refused to make a complaint. The company took advice which resulted in no further action as it would have been unfair to the alleged perpetrator. Thankfully in this case as the girl in question was totally untrustworthy and had ulterior motives i.e. discrediting her colleague.
- However, that was many years ago. Less than one year ago I became aware of a very similar incident and the advice given to HR was that they had no other choice but to take things further. HR were told if anything came out in the future, they could be viewed as delinquent in their duties towards staff. How complicated is this? Especially if the person making the claim is lying or exaggerating.

CHAPTER TWELVE
Men in Tights

A few years ago, a new product was launched, the self-tanning ladies' tights. Brilliant invention apparently. An elderly lady heard about them and decided to order a few pairs online.

Unfortunately for her, she did not have an email account or a credit card, so she asked her genuinely nice obliging son in law, Jimmy to purchase them online for her. Jimmy diligently placed the order and forgot about it, but not for long. Fast forward three weeks and Jimmy was delivering an important presentation to the entire company from his laptop when an instant message popped up to let him know his three pairs of size medium ladies, self-tanning tights were being delivered the following day. As his back was to the screen, Jimmy kept talking about supply chain management while sniggers went around the room until he figured out what had happened. It was even funnier to see Jimmy struggling to get the mouse to remove the offending message. The dangers of mixing home and work emails strikes again but more importantly the risks of using your laptop for live demos.

I heard too from Hannah who used her laptop to deliver her very professional PowerPoint presentation about digital marketing strategies. Someone in the audience piped up and asked Hannah if she could she open a rival company's website to compare it. Big, big mistake as Hannah the night before had been on a very naughty website ordering some goodies for the upcoming hen night she was going to. Loads of giggles and sniggers again and years later Hannah is still known as "hand cuff Hannah".

Lessons learned

- Always disable pop ups and instant messages while giving company presentations.
- Keep the surfing and home shopping to the home laptop or tablet.
- Buy your mother in law some fake tan so she does not need the self-tanning tights.
- The list of hilarious and not so hilarious pop ups on screens at meetings is endless, some of my favourites,
  o A developer who messaged his manager "Don't show them the demo of the new software, it is still full of bugs", while the customer was sitting there.
  o A guy who was running late for a meeting, did not realise it had started and messaged his colleague "give me ten minutes, gotta poop", straight up on the screen in the meeting.
  o Years ago when I worked in Intel, the Site lead would take questions on stage from any of the workforce at the annual town hall, I remember him being asked via message " How do you feel about Take That breaking up?". He pretty much ended the meeting saying that "people weren't taking the meeting seriously enough".
  o A manager presenting to the senior team when one of his male staff messaged him describing all the terrible symptoms of his man flu. The females in the room found it extremely amusing as he described his symptoms in great detail while his manager tried to kill the conversation on the screen in front of everyone.
  o A wife who messaged her husband at work that she was going to kill him for forgetting to bring the bins out again, during a live demo.

CHAPTER THIRTEEN
Rock and Scroll

Denise was exhausted, she had just returned to work after an utterly fabulous weekend in Dublin. Not only had she seen her favourite band REM, but she had also met a fabulous man, Rob and had what can only be described as a filthy weekend with him. She was smiling away as they both exchanged emails, yes, she was using her work one but she knew management didn't monitor email. This continued for a few days and then things went quiet. Life resorted to normal and work continued in her phone support role. Then out of the blue, Rob the love interest emailed her a particularly funny joke, something about a thermos being mixed up with a vibrator, which Denise immediately forwarded to her entire department on their social email channel.

Less than five minutes later, one of her colleagues stood up and screamed – "DENISE FORGOT TO SCROLL DOWN" and there it was for all to see, the smutty email exchange detailing what they had done, should have done and were definitely going to do when they met up next, which for all you romantics out there never happened again.

This is one of the funnier email forwarding stories, so many of them revolve around Person A responding to a group message, bitching about Person B and then finding out that, Person B, was copied on it in the first place! No easy way to get out of that one other than to apologise or claim you knew all along they were copied in the first place - stinks of desperation though!

- Always scroll down, never blindly forward an email, you never know what is lurking underneath.
- Know your company's policy on BCC (Blind Copy), some companies forbid the use of it as it is deemed to be sneaky.
- If you do find use for a strawberry cornetto, other than eating it, do not tell your entire workforce.

Did you know you can buy email software that will give you incredible search capabilities? If there is a legal case and you want to search for every conversation on your company server including DELETED emails that mention key words, you can get a listing in minutes.

No email is ever deleted. Please remember that.

I recall a female in an organisation accused her manager of sexually harassing her, the email software that HR used brought up a list of all their conversations and guess what – they were having an affair for six months and he went back to the wife. She was trying to ger her revenge on the cheating pig! She lost her job and he got promoted to CEO within a year. However, without the software the CEO could have had his career destroyed. He may have been a cheating rat but the lady in question was no better, she was willing to destroy him.

CHAPTER FOURTEEN
The Camera Doesn't Lie

Bethany was delighted with her new laptop, it was fast, it was light and the fact that it didn't have a camera didn't faze her in the slightest. She had never used a laptop camera and had no intentions of doing so.

It was a busy Thursday and Bethany decided to work from home. While dialling into the weekly call with her design team she got a call from a customer to see if she could meet them at short notice.

Bethany, being a great multitasker figured she better get out of her pyjamas and get dressed and put on some make up. All of this was done while she stayed on the design team call.

The next day Bethany was talking to IT support and one of the guys complimented her laptop and told her it had one of the best cameras for its size. Bethany went white and nearly threw up, she literally thought she had undressed and redressed in her bedroom while on video in front of the management team. Horror! Luckily, this time she hadn't but she could have. Bethany had failed to realise the tiny new pin hole at the top of her laptop was a camera that luckily for her was not on.

Lessons learned

- Know your tech and like a lot of tech people and celebrities, cover your camera.
- Do not from work in your PJs.

CHAPTER FIFTEEN
Maybe Baby?

Alan was at an especially important sales meeting; his performance was not great the previous quarter, so he was nervous. So nervous that he went in and out of the bathroom quite a few times. Alan was in the meeting with HR, his manager and most of the senior team as this meeting was crucial to figure out cash flow and hire needs for the coming quarter.

The meeting was going relatively ok and Alan excused himself to go to the bathroom. No sooner had he left the room than his phone kept sending out an annoying alert sound, his very annoyed Manager picked the phone up to try and turn off the alert, only to find it was a "Congratulations you are ovulating" message from his wife's app that he was connected to. Alan returned and a few minutes later, the phone started alerting again, he lifted it up to turn it off and was suitably mortified. However, he could see from the mixture of faces opposite him that everyone else knew what was going on. He continued with the meeting but couldn't concentrate for many reasons!

Apps are great, alerts are great but keep them out of the workplace, I have heard stories of people's positive chlamydia tests, reminders to attend STI clinics, vasectomy follow up appointments all popping up on people's phones in the workplace and worst of all people's screen savers being very intimate photos.

Lessons learned

- Manage your phone alerts VERY carefully!

CHAPTER SIXTEEN
Induction, Seduction

I have so many stories concerning dating online and how it impacts the workplace, they could fill a book of their own.

Take Julian for example, it was his first start-up and the pressure was on big time. He had made a recent hire called Mark and it was Mark's first day. Mark was a good looking, well presented young man who had relocated to take this new job as a senior software tester. Mark was apprehensive about moving to a new town, but he had a long-term girlfriend Julie in the new town and he would not be lonely.

So, on the first day of his new role Mark arrived in the office, completely dishevelled, rough and quite smelly.

Julian was appalled, he had interviewed Mark and was excited to have him join the team. Being a frank and honest person Julian pretty much asked him what the hell was going on and that he looked like a train wreck! Mark explained that he had relocated to be with his girlfriend Julie in her hometown but that he had decided the previous week to have one last fling. He had gone on Tinder, met a girl called Tonya and spent the night with her in a Dublin hotel. Unknown or probably too drunk to remember, there was a series of photos taken in the hotel of their encounter. Mark never contacted Tonya again. As she had no details of him, she could not get in touch, she was ghosted. However, the night before Mark's new job, Tonya was snooping on Facebook and found a post from Julie. Julie had posted the most romantic pics of herself and Mark and was announcing to the world that they were moving in together. Tonya went nuts and private messaged Julie and told her all about the night in the hotel and sent her on the pics to prove that they were doing a lot more than talking.

So, that same night Mark arrived at Julie's house, car packed up and ready to start his new job. He was met by an irate Julie. They had a massive fight and Mark ended up sleeping in his car, too scared to leave his prize possessions – vinyl records, all 300 of them unattended overnight.

Back to Julian who remember is doing a start-up and has a to do list a mile long. He must now sit and listen to this entire story in place of the standard company induction.

This story did not end well for anyone, Mark lasted about 4 weeks, gave in his notice. Julian was back to advertising and chasing a refund from the recruiter who placed Mark and generally loosing huge momentum in the business.

Mark also gave a scathing review of Julian to the US head office at his exit interview despite all the help he got and management time he consumed. I am sure if he looks back now, he will realise how embarrassing his behaviour was in a brand-new job.

Lessons learned

- From Julian's point of view, if someone does not take their first day seriously, do not waste a month on them. While it is nice to be helpful to your staff, do not waste time on a situation that is not going to be resolved. If you are in a start-up, every minute matters and there aren't enough hours in the day. Do not waste time on time wasters.
- Know the small print of recruitment contracts, it is expensive to use recruiters, so know what happens if the employee does not work out and you have paid a hefty fee. It is too late to start looking for full refunds if your contract with the recruitment firm says otherwise.

CHAPTER SEVENTEEN
Captain Underpants

Trish was extremely popular in the team. She was young free and single and a big Tinder fan. While some people might not broadcast this, Trish had no problem and her team seemed to be very well briefed on her liaisons. Trish worked shift and was often in the office alone at night and yes you have guessed it, she brought her Tinder dates to the office. As she was a great worker, no one would have guessed from her output that she had been anyway distracted. So how did she get caught out?

One day after Trish's latest hook up there was a flood in the ladies' toilet so a plumber was called out. After a very short investigation a pair of men's pink briefs were recovered that had been flushed down the ladies' loo but had got caught and blocked it. Blocked it and the resultant flood had not only flooded the office toilets but leaked through the ceiling and all over the awfully expensive 3 in one copier, printer, scanner in the office below.
An insurance claim had to made for Eur 25,000 to repair the ceiling, replace the equipment below and replace carpets.

As Trish had been the last to use the loos, she confessed and said that they were too nervous to use the office because of the CCTV so used the bathroom for their encounter. An incredibly beautiful story, I often wondered did she get married and share it with their children and maybe with the guests at the wedding during the wedding speech!

Trish was dismissed and left quietly. What was really shocking was that she had brought several different men that she barely knew into an office, given them access codes to come up to her, pardon the pun and let them know the run of the office. How that office wasn't ransacked is a miracle.

This story is awfully familiar nowadays and many managers have shared similar stories with me.

One founder told me that they found out an employee's boyfriend had been evicted from his rented apartment and he was sleeping in his girlfriend's office from midnight to 6 am for several months before he got caught. The support team was small and they were all in on the secret as it was only meant to be for a few nights. He was only caught when an operations manager arrived in at 6am to set up the conference room for a meeting only to find someone asleep on an air bed in the corner.

If Trish had been caught on CCTV with her visitors, that evidence could probably not have been used against her. CCTV policies must be detailed and you need to explain the reason for CCTV and let employees know why it is being installed in the organisation. In this instance the company put up CCTV but did not have any policies around usage, so Trish if dismissed on CCTV evidence could have taken the company to the Workplace Relations Commission and potentially been reinstated.

Lessons learned

- Lone workers need to be trusted but checked on too.
- The danger of access codes is that they can be given out to people. One office I knew was robbed when an ex-boyfriend took the access code and alarm code from his girlfriend's phone and broke in looking for cash. There was no CCTV and he was only caught when a neighbouring business called the police who caught him red handed.
- If disposing of your underwear, remember everything is recoverable in both Technology and in Toilets.

CHAPTER EIGHTEEN
An Affair to Remember

Linda was extremely nervous about her first day, she had been up early, extra effort with hair, makeup and clothes. Although the new company was huge, she had been reassured at the interviews that the department she was joining was small enough and had a good team that got on very well.

The first few hours were easy enough, a lovely HR person had walked her through policies and an induction video, and she was then scheduled to meet with her new manager. As she walked into her new manager's office all she could think of was how this job really needed to work out. Linda had just re-mortgaged and bought a swanky bigger apartment with a great view. The HR manager introduced her to Frank and apologised for all the balloons and cards in the office welcoming Frank's new baby girl into the world. Linda had not met Frank the financial controller as he had been on paternity leave, but she had met the other accountants she would be working with.

Frank stretched out his hand to greet her (this was pre COVID-19 after all) and she had a flashback of Frank and herself in the backseat of Frank's Audi less than a week ago. OMG, she had met Frank online, hooked up several times but Frank told her he was Gerry. Frank was unphased and she genuinely did not know if he recognised her until the HR manager left.

Awkward does not begin to describe how she felt. He immediately apologised for lying about his name, "forget the name" she said, "what about your wife and baby?".

To cut a long story very short, Linda never passed her probation in the company. Apparently, she didn't fit the culture. Despite getting on with work, doing a great job and never ever mentioning Audi gymnastics to Frank, he got rid of her. Her best friend told her to go to HR or to go to a lawyer, but for what, she felt everyone in a relatively small town would think she was a home wrecker.

Instead, Linda got another job, a lesser paid job and really struggled for a couple of years. When she heard Frank's, marriage broke up she was secretly delighted.

Lessons learned

- The biggest lesson here is that if you know you will not be able to work with your manager / employee end it sooner rather than later. Life is way too short to go to work worried and stressed. If you can get out, do so and move on. I would have far more time for someone at interview if they explained a short stint at a company as one that was a bad match and they knew there was no future so left, rather than someone who stuck it out for a year or two miserable. I find nowadays that people are very frank during interviews about explaining short stays in companies or when explaining gaps on their CVs. If someone is rehearsing answers, you do tend to know they are lying whereas someone being articulate and honest is far more likely to land them the job. If someone has multiple short stays in companies and blames the company every time, that is a totally different story.
- If some guy only wants to meet you in his Audi and never wants to go somewhere public, be suspicious!

CHAPTER NINETEEN
Background Chequered

When you think about references, they are kind of ridiculous. Of course, people are going to give you the name of someone who will tell you how great they are and how they would recommend them to any employer. No one is going to give you the name of someone who will confirm they were a lazy slob who robbed the stationery and seldom made any effort.

Geraldine learned this the hard way when she hired a friend of one of her neighbours to do a junior accounts role that was open. His name was Ralph and he seemed like a good worker. He adapted very quickly to the role but Ralph was very vague about why his last role didn't work out. Apparently, he was let go by his manager for no reason. However, Geraldine had a million and one things to do with the company take over that was happening, so she ignored that little voice in the back of her head. Ralph seemed to be doing the job ok, he wasn't brilliant, but it was one less role to fill and Geraldine was moving through other tasks.

One day Geraldine had to reprimand Ralph for something minor, he had forgot to collect a visitor from a local hotel on his way to work as agreed. Geraldine gave him some feedback about how unprofessional this was. It was no big deal, and like all feedback Geraldine very much framed the feedback to help Ralph, or so she thought.

Nothing could prepare Geraldine for what came next, Ralph became nasty beyond belief - he became openly hostile, he put up cryptic social media blogs and he generally behaved like a sulky teenager. The passive aggressive Facebook posts are becoming all too common with younger staff and most CEOs I chat with tell me that the minute someone is let go, they know the Facebook posts will start. Geraldine learned the hard way why Ralph's prior job had not gone well, if she had tracked down his previous employer for a chat, she could have saved herself a lot of grief.

What was very sad about it was that Ralph had huge potential, he had a wife and two small children relying on his income, but he simply was not mature enough to take any feedback.

Lessons learned

- Never ever ever ever ever ever hire someone without doing every possible check on the person that you can do formally and informally.
- Always listen to your inner voice that knows best, so many situations in this book could have been avoided if the managers in question listened to their gut feelings on a person or a situation.
- I have said it again in other chapters, use the probation period to weed out the weeds, harsh as that may sound. Nearly everyone will pass probations as they will really want the job at hand and be very good at it, but occasionally you can meet lazy people who will not mirror the culture that you want to cultivate. Nearly every seminar on Employment Legislation I go to these days emphasise this point, if in doubt extend the probation period because when an employee is permanent it is so much harder to part company.
- If you operate a behavioural style of interview you can ask questions that look for real examples e.g. "describe a time you had to deal with a confrontational customer". This way you get an insight into the candidate's skill set, emotional maturity, work experience and values. This can prove invaluable and prevent you hiring a bad candidate.

CHAPTER TWENTY
Culture Eats Strategy

Matt was a fabulous programmer. He could do the work of at least five regular programmers. This is quite unique to software. In finance, a good accountant might do the work of two average accountants, but in software you do often come across some super performers. The problem was that Matt was "an arse". He had the unique ability to annoy and upset virtually everyone he came across. However, he always got the jobs he wanted, he did them fast and good and kept the revenues coming in.

As time went on a growing resentment of him was palpable in the company. The rest of the staff felt annoyed that he could be rude, late, condescending etc. but still be allowed to pick and choose the projects he worked on. He was pass remarkable about other people's abilities and he regularly spoke negatively about management. To make matters worse, he would socialise with customers and fill them in on all the company issues that should have remained confidential. Three companies had a Matt (Note - all software companies have at least one Matt),

Company A
Company A were struggling with cash flow and needed to grow their customer base fast, so they kept Matt happy. He came and went as he pleased, he said what he wanted to people and on staff nights out he barely hid his coke habit. At one senior management meeting several of the team felt it was time to call it a day with him. He had yet again been late into work and did not attend the weekly team meeting. The HR manager spoke about the impact he was having on the rest of the staff. She was routinely getting feedback that there was a growing resentment towards management from the rest of the staff who were fed up with his special treatment. The

HR leader was overruled, and Matt was kept on. Within two years, at least five staff had left citing Matt as the main reason for their decision. That is a lot of intellectual capital for a company to lose and the cost of five replacements was enormous. Speaking to the CEO he was full of regrets and said if he had his time again Matt would not have passed his probation period - apparently during probation he voiced to a German colleague that all Germans were boring and not as capable as Irish workers. Yikes.

Company B
Company B had a Matt but company B were very bought into their company values and culture and Matt did not embody many of their values. Apart from a technical team lead everyone wanted to end Matt's employment with their company, so they did, he was disciplined for insulting the marketing manager. The fallout was considerable, Matt having been escorted out of the building did not take long to bitch to customers, suppliers, fellow colleagues and he also made a claim for unfair dismissal which he lost. The cost was high, and the CEO severely regretted ever hiring the guy.

Company C
Company C was a start-up whose CEO Eoghan had been around the block a few times and had several start-ups under his belt. Eoghan knew very quickly what Matt was, but he also knew he had to get beta versions of platforms built very quickly. Eoghan indulged Matt with pay, bonus, holidays and flexible hours but Eoghan made one significant decision and that was to give Matt two junior software engineers to mentor and get up to speed. Matt loved having direct reports and felt very important. More importantly for the company, Matt's subordinates came up to speed within a year and knew Matt's projects inside out. When the inevitable bust up came, and they always do with a Matt, the company survived and had two exceptional engineers left behind. The bust up was ridiculous, Matt had without management approval stayed an

extra two days at an engineering conference he attended and missed a major company deadline, when cautioned for this he went nuts and stormed out. Good riddance.

Lessons learned

- Never compromise your culture and values for the sake of one maverick, in the end they will cost you more.
- Listen to HR, they are trained and know the long-term consequences of bad behaviour. Sometimes in organisations the CFO will command a lot of respect for pointing out where the company is heading financially and the forecast will be expressed in monetary terms but when HR point out the consequences of behaviour they don't always talk to the economic impact which is easier to understand and they don't get taken as seriously.

"Culture eats strategy for breakfast"
a phrase made famous by Peter Drucker
is a reality.
Any company disconnecting the two are putting their company's success at risk.

I remember starting work at a multinational whose mission statement and values were remarkable and I related to them immediately. Within a week I found out that there was no substance to them, the senior team were so divided and spoke disparagingly of each other to their staff, that was within a week! It is like walking into a house where you just know the couple were killing each other five minutes before you enter, you can feel the atmosphere and cannot hide it (Father Ted fans' think John and Mary).

CHAPTER TWENTY-ONE
Prince Charming

Kevin was often described as "a ride". He was truly tall, dark and handsome and was very charming. Boy did he trade on his looks but he was a very average performer and seemed to be able to twist men and women around his little finger.

In next to no time he was having his second fling in the office however this time it was with a subordinate called Suzanne. They barely hid their liaison, giggling, taking hour long lunch breaks together every day, going wherever they went without inviting anyone along. Senior leaders chose to ignore the relationship. While not official, everyone seemed to know they were a couple.

Kevin was single and enjoying life very much. The fling with Suzanne appeared to fizzle out and they both seemed cool enough with each other and life continued on as normal. The following year the company's finances started to suffer, their products weren't selling well, and it was time for layoffs. Suzanne was selected for redundancy, her job as a fulltime digital marketer was pretty much now all done online in a few hours by the head of marketing who also reported to Kevin.

Suzanne unlike her relationship with Kevin did not take this lying down! She very quickly made a claim that the CEO selected her and not Kevin for the axe due to their relationship. To ensure the case did not make any headlines Suzanne ended up getting a large cash pay-out in return for signing a non-disclosure agreement. The company had managed to incur large costs by turning a blind eye to what was going on and the departure of the HR manager a few months later was rumoured to be linked to the pay-out.

- Ignore affairs at your peril, they will bite you, particularly between subordinates and managers.
- Stormy Daniels NDA did not work out too well for all concerned.

The Irish Independent Newspaper reported in November 2011 that a third of all office workers admit to mixing business with pleasure, the same article states

"If policies are in place and guidelines written into office codes of conduct, then that makes it easier to deal with problems should they arise."

Glamour Magazine and www.lawyers.com sponsored a survey in 2017 and the finding were that 41% of employed Americans ages 25 to 40 admitted to having engaged in an office romance.

CHAPTER TWENTY-TWO
Radio GA GA

Dee was thrilled to hear her company was expanding and creating over two hundred new jobs and furthermore the company had acquired a local supplier which was a further seventy jobs. Dee was running the Irish branch of a US multinational and she loved the role, she also had responsibility for the UK offices, but loved being in Ireland far more. Dee knew the announcement would mean far more time for her in Ireland.

There was a huge day planned for the announcement, the list of dignitaries was impressive for the announcement lunch, the mayor, local politicians, journalists and a TV crew. It was hard to keep it quiet and only a handful of people knew about the impending announcement.

However - Dee was invited to talk on a panel on the local radio station. A weekly radio business show was going to be talking about gender pay gaps and she was one of three firms invited as she had also written a book on the subject in college.

Yes, you guessed it, the inevitable happened. Dee managed to spill the beans about the announcement. It just kind of came out of her mouth when asked a question about how many workers she employed in the firm.

Before Dee knew it, she was on calls to the US being reprimanded for the announcement, several of the politicians pulled out of the launch day as they knew the story would be old news and would get limited coverage. Dee discovered the corporate disease of "Recency", anyone who has worked for multinationals or very large organisations will be familiar with this particular affliction. Despite working incredibly hard for the company and making huge personal sacrifices, one mistake and she was effectively demoted. This was a quite simple mistake to make but the consequences were enormous, and it illustrates how important it is to prepare for radio or TV if you aren't used to them.

Lessons learned

- Failure to prepare means prepare to fail.
- Know your local radio journalists, they can sniff out a story and trade on the fact that you might be a little bit nervous sitting in front of them.
- Do not be afraid to spend money on consultants, there are consultants for everything these days and they are experts in their fields. If you need to prep staff for TV, Radio, Podcasts or general marketing train your staff, it is a very worthwhile investment as your brand is usually very valuable and very important to your company. The story above is harmless but remember the Ratner effect.

Gerald Ratner inherited his father's jewellery business in 1984 and turned it into a multimillion-dollar empire within a decade. (H Samuel, Ernst Jones). Asked how it was possible for his company to be selling a sherry decanter for the amazing price of £4.95 he answered

"How can you sell this for such a low price? I say, "because it's total crap."

He said this at a speech at the Institute of Directors Dinner in 1991. Shares then collapsed, he lost 2,500 shops and became know in the tabloids as "Gerald Crapner".

CHAPTER TWENTY-THREE
Jay's Fluids

Benji was from Germany and had joined his first Irish software firm. Benji had excellent English and could communicate extremely well with the team, however Benji did not seem to be progressing in the company as fast as he should have. Despite being talented and able his manager did not however feel he was learning quickly enough. The HR lead had tried to intervene several times but felt he did not really get to grips with what was going on. Just before a year in the company Benji's probation period was extended and he was extremely upset. He phoned in sick and was not seen for a few days. Upon his return Charles the HR lead had a long chat with him and finally penetrated Benji's calm exterior. Benji claimed that at every quarterly review he was being told his work was ok. He claimed he had never been given poor feedback. Charles was confused at this and immediately met with Benji's line manager Karen. Karen described how she felt she did give solid feedback to Benji but she was a very positive person and didn't feel it necessary to be too hard or too direct.

Bingo! Karen had been doing it the Irish way – "Your work is …(pause)… ok" said with a grimace. No negative feedback was directly conveyed.

In Ireland we do not have a word for No (or YES) in the Irish language. If asked did you go the shop in Irish, the answer would be "yes, I did go" or "no I did not go". We communicate with the verb.

Additionally, the Irish language has a fraction of the amount of words that the German or English language has, we rely a lot on body language, that grimace, that gritting of the teeth etc.

Sidebar, many sociologists believe this to be the reason that Irish people generally integrate into other cultures very quickly as we read humans cues innately.
So poor Benji was not picking up on Karen's messages that his work was ok average, not ok good.

Several of the CEOs told me while writing this book that they struggle with performance reviews for people where English was not their first language. They found that using a good paper-based system with forms and comments was far better than just relying on chats.

Please note that very few of us in Ireland speak Irish daily, despite a huge percentage of the population circa 40% being able to speak Irish but we have Irish in our genes as we only stopped speaking it a few hundred years ago.

Lessons learned

- Be very mindful of language differences and go out of your way to compensate so that all staff are treated equally. Particularly when you are giving negative feedback to staff it is imperative that they grasp what you are saying so that they can work to improve performance.
- Be careful when using slang with staff during formal meetings as it can lead to confusion. I remember a US visitor losing their luggage and asking an Irish colleague where he could buy a few pairs of pants, of course he meant trousers but the Irish guy thought it was underpants. I also heard of a very unfortunate mix up with Jeyes Fluid and Jay's Fluids!

CHAPTER TWENTY-FOUR
Brass Neck

Laurence was a strange guy; he did not have any close friends at work, but he did a lot of overtime and cover for others. This made him quite valuable to the company that was in its infancy and needed everyone pulling their weight. He was very prone to telling exaggerated stories around the office and he was very often caught out in lies, which for anyone dealing with staff on probation, big red flag. However, he did his job well and his work could not be faulted.

One day Laurence did not come into work, he rang in, apparently, he had slipped putting out the bins and hurt his arm. He explained in great detail that he had gone to the local hospital and stayed the night before being released with a sling. However, when asked, he had no paperwork to back up his story but said he would be able to get paperwork in a few days' time.

His team leader Gerald did not believe Laurence as the story didn't add up. Gerald did remember that there was a tracking device for mileage on Laurence's company car so Gerald checked it out and sure enough, the software showed Laurence had used the car the previous night and indeed several times since he rang work, in agony from his sick bed!

Gerald wanted to know the truth, after all he was trying to grow the office and win more business. So, Gerald emailed Laurence and asked him to come into work for a chat and guess what? - Laurence turned up, very nervous with a ridiculous looking homemade sling, claiming he had got a taxi there and would be getting one home.

Gerald listened to the story about the slip and then confronted Laurence, he brought up the software program on his PC showing that Laurence's car was parked 2 streets away and not at his home over thirty miles away.

Laurence denied, denied, denied the allegations but eventually broke down crying, claiming he was stressed and could not cope with the role he had taken on. In this instance both parties realised that the situation was not resolvable, and they agreed to part ways amicably.

Never underestimate what a bad employee can do and never underestimate what a savvy manager can do.

Lessons learned

- Tracking devices will track you! "Simples!". Similarly claiming you were out sick and stressed but your Facebook shows you drunk in temple bar is also not a good career move. More often than not, it is your fellow teammates that will hang you out to dry and not your manager perusing your social media accounts.
- Big companies have big budgets and regularly use private investigators to investigate fraudulent claims. The news will regularly show an employee taking part in races but claiming in court they could barely walk and then they are exposed as cheats and liars.
- If faking an injury, make sure your props are up to scratch.
- If people in the organisation are going to such extremes to avoid work maybe it is time to look at what stress the company is putting the person under and what supports could be offered. Maybe you should embrace a company wellness program, there are plenty of inexpensive solutions for companies out there.

CHAPTER TWENTY-FIVE
Video Killed the Radio Star

Luke was a tough factory owner and had no hesitation taking on problems. He was certain that thefts from his factory were happening on the night shift so he installed CCTV. About three weeks later he spent his weekend checking footage and caught four employees stealing radio parts that they manufactured on site.

Luke was furious, not only did he know these employees but he also knew their families. During the last recession he had re-mortgaged his house to prop up his business and keep these guys in jobs. Yet here he was, watching the four of them systematically putting parts into the boots of their cars.

Luke was outraged but calmed down over the weekend. His initial reaction was to go to the Police, get a lawyer but he did not want all the bad publicity and the court case that he thought would ensue. Luke's wife begged him to get legal advice but he would not listen, he was old school, he could deal with this. Or so he thought!

On Monday night he headed to the factory, called the four men into his office, showed them the footage that he had downloaded to his phone and calmly asked the four of them to leave and never come back. The men in question said nothing, they were shocked and pretty much just walked.

Two days later, still reeling from the betrayal Luke opened his post and found that the four "beauties" had gone to a law firm and were now seeking their jobs back due to unfair dismissal. Why? Well - CCTV policies must be very detailed and employers need to explain the reason for CCTV and let their employees know why they have them. In this company's case the management put up CCTV but did not have any policies around them nor any signs saying they were there.

Luke was beside himself with anger. He waited for the relevant legal hearing and he lost his case and had to reinstate the four men. Two years later Luke sold the business and moved to early retirement in Spain. His wife said he never ever got over the betrayal. The missing parts amounted to over ninety thousand euro over eighteen months.

Lessons learned

- Hire a HR person or agency on a full time or part time basis. The solutions out there are not as expensive as you might think and in the long run will end up saving you money and not costing you money. What is very expensive is fighting legal challenges as you will have to pay a legal firm and generally rates are very high indeed.
- Have a thorough company handbook and update it regularly. It is no use putting effort into a company handbook if you are not going to keep it updated and more importantly follow your own rules. At any legal hearing, the first thing to be checked will be, did your company follow its own documented rules and procedures. If you did not, how could you expect your workers to.
- Always pay your night shift workers an occasional night-time visit.
- If CCTV is being installed for staff and property security on your premises and someone objects to it, be concerned!

CHAPTER TWENTY-SIX
Divorce Court

We have all heard the saying that the most stressful life events are death, moving to a new house and divorce. Ellen certainly learned this the hard way. Ellen hired a marketer Matthew; Matthew started the job with gusto and Ellen was happy that he could implement all the marketing strategies that she knew her business needed.

Very soon after starting in his role Matthew started leaving work earlier and earlier and sometimes, he arrived late. Matthew confessed that he had cheated on his wife, met a girl on a dating app and moved in with her in less than three months of his twenty-year marriage breaking up. Added to the mix was custody of his two children which was beyond complicated.

At every business meeting Matthew ended up talking about his personal life and feeling deeply sorry for himself. Worse still Ellen discovered that he was endlessly telling his staff every personal detail about his new romance like a love-struck teenager. The staff were beyond embarrassed. Ellen spoke to him and tried to make him realise how inappropriate his behaviour was and how if he wasn't careful his performance would start to slip. Matthew very rapidly went from a good strong performer to a below average performer who nobody in the company really wanted anything to do with.

The problem for Ellen now was that she wanted to help Matthew and really did not want to add to his woes by firing him. How wrong she was, as Matthew continued to non-perform and despite meeting after meeting with HR, he failed to deliver results. The final straw came when one Wednesday Ellen met Matthew's wife at a random charity fashion show where they both knew the organiser. The ex-wife was terribly upset that Matthew was seeking custody for some weekdays of their children. Clearly, Matthew was not looking after the children any day during weekdays. Ellen felt terrible let down as she had for six months allowed Matthew to finish early to look after his children, three evenings a week. This was the final straw for Ellen and she took Matthew through the full disciplinary process which took months and months and was torturous before he was fired.

The sad part of this story Ellen said was that it made her hard, she had really tried to work with Matthew but he had abused her trust and abused the company's goodwill. Instead of trying to excel in a new career he wallowed in his own mess. I heard later that he split with his new girlfriend, as Dr Phil would say "If he does it with you, he'll do it to you". Harsh but true.

Lessons learned

- ☺ If you have a staff member going through a tough time, help them out with formal supports. Many health policies offer counselling and many company doctors will offer counselling services - do not become your employees' counsellor. You will not be thanked by anyone for it.
- ☺ Many CEOs have told me that a person's character is especially important and if someone will cheat on their spouse, they will cheat on their employer too. I personally don't agree with this as often employees can immerse themselves in their job to block out personal issues and can be super productive.
- ☺ Engage HR if staff are struggling so that they can get help but still behave professionally on the job.
- ☺ Common sense should tell you if you join a start-up you will be expected to give 100% so think before you join one. Your head needs to be in the game.

CHAPTER TWENTY-SEVEN
Toxic Dump

If anyone reading this has had a toxic employee, a truly toxic employee they will already be in a cold sweat having read this sentence. I remember years ago reading how multinationals will pay off toxic people and get rid of them. "This cannot be true" I thought, "how poor are their HR people" that was before I had my first true toxic employee. Nothing and I mean nothing can prepare you for what a truly toxic employee can do. They are like a virus that infects everything and everyone around them.

Do not think you can buy them over, do not even try. Do not think that they have a conscience like a normal person, they do not. Do not think that they will respond to opportunities and being part of a good team.

The truly toxic person will find a way to hate anyone they perceive as "management" no matter what is done for them. They will trust nobody and will behave like the bullies that they are. If you are reading this and thinking - I could handle one, I could turn them around, you are deluded. The truly toxic employee basically does not want to be in work, they are either there because they must be or their spouse made them. They will drain every ounce of life out of you. You will also be in a state of disbelief that such awful people actually exist on this planet.

Lazy people can be worked on and bad time keeping can be improved but the toxic employee will corrode your organisation from the inside out. Often it will be too late before you even recognise who this person is. They have a way of infecting those around them. Before you know it a team that were once trustworthy, energised and nice to be around will start questioning everything you do, they will no longer put the company first and there will be a terrible atmosphere around them.

Can you do anything? Yes, you can – get rid of them. Simple as that. You may have reasons to keep them on, for example, a deluded sense that things will get better but they will not. Fear that you will have to find a hire to replace them - bring it on.

Luckily, there are very very few of these toxic employees around and hopefully you will get through your career without encountering one. Signs to look out for are,

- An inflated sense of their own abilities
- An unwillingness to share information
- A distrust of all authority
- An inability to take personal responsibility for their behaviours, actions, work and results
- Everyone in the world is to blame for everything except themselves
- Bullying behaviour
- Superficially nice to colleagues, managers and team leaders but behind their backs is ripping them apart

The CEOs I have spoken to say they see an anger in the toxic employee that is often just below the surface and leaks out occasionally. These people also seem to believe that everyone is out to get them and that someone else is always to blame for anything that goes wrong in their lives. Sometimes they exhibit sexual deviancy that can surface in the workplace as sexual harassment. The CEOs that I spoke to who had toxic employees spoke of their multiple affairs, boasting about their affairs, an attraction to minors and an over inflated sense of how attractive they were.

Many years ago, I had the displeasure of working with such a toxic employee who assaulted a fellow employee on a work night out and was dismissed

The toxic employees literally would fail to recognise themselves as a toxic employee from the description above, which demonstrates their utter lack of self-awareness.

Lessons learned

- If you encounter a toxic employee, engage HR or outside services and get rid of them, your health and your staff do not deserve such a work colleague.
- Remember during your worst hours that you will one day be rid of them but they are stuck with themselves forever.
- Do not believe every Facebook post you read which implies all bad employees are the result of bad managers or that you can always teach an old dog new tricks. Sometimes in life you can't teach an old dog new tricks.

"Toxic people attach themselves like cinder blocks tied to your ankles, and then invite you for a swim in their poisoned waters."
— **John Mark Green**

CHAPTER TWENTY-EIGHT
The Shaper

Every multinational has a few "shapers" and the bigger the company the more shapers there are. Shapers throw the right shapes at the right people and get on. Eamon was such a shaper; he was the king of managing up. His colleagues knew how lazy he was, his staff knew that he always took credit for their work but the senior team loved him. He had a way of worming his way around the senior team, long before he joined it.

Never underestimate a shaper and never think they are stupid. It takes considerable skill to work in a busy environment and do very little but get on very well. They suddenly are playing the same sport as the CEO; they suddenly are in the gym at lunchtime next to the CFO or in Eamon's case he joined the company golf society and regularly got to play with the CEO.

Shapers are not bad people; in fact, they are very nice people and get on with everyone. Their staff do not particularly dislike them, Eamon's team all thought he was a nice guy, just lazy. Eamon like most shapers knew and played the annual performance appraisal system. He knew the timing, the people who would give feedback on him and he knew the key things he needed to do to get promoted and he gave them all his efforts. If you join a large firm and you encounter a shaper, sit back and take note because it is a skill set all of its own.

If your goal is to be paid well, not kill yourself with effort, become a shaper. I have worked for five multinationals and I can still think of great shapers in all of them. Interestingly most of them are men. Most women will not be surprised to hear this.

- I am a great believer that hard work means the cream always rises to the top but some people can definitely fast track their rise to the top.
- Maybe with social media, it is no harm to do the odd spy on your boss and figure out what their interests are, but word of caution - try not to like a post from three years ago on their Facebook page.
- If you are working for a company that you feel does not value you, or that people are overtaking you, do something about it. Always start by talking to your manager, then to HR. You might get some feedback on yourself that is hard to hear, but at least you will know what the reasons are for your lack of progression. If you have tried this and genuinely feel that your company has its favourites etc. move on. There are lots of other companies out there that might value you more and if you stay in your current position and begin to feel resentment, you won't be doing your best work and you won't be happy. Also, consider a start-up - if you have a great idea and have been thinking about it for years, go for it. There are now more supports than ever before for people to start their own business. In the Southeast we are blessed with inexpensive shared workspace options if you cannot work from home for any reason and a community of entrepreneurs only too willing to help. The brilliance of a not too big city is that you can get to know a lot of businesspeople quite quickly and you will find a sense of community among them.

CHAPTER TWENTY-NINE
Stink Bomb

Dave was lovely but Dave was smelly. No one wanted to work near him. His colleagues tried a few times to hint at the situation. Spare deodorant was left in the bathroom, on the shared service desk etc. but Dave did not take the hint. In winter, his coat smelled like something found in a sewer. As a fifty something year old man it was hard to believe he had been in the workplace for as long as he had, and still remain smelly. There was no easy way around this - Dave's manager Sheila had to talk to him.

These conversations are mortifying. They are bad for the smelly one, but a million times worse for the HR person who has to sit across a desk from them and have such an excruciating conversation. No one wants to have these conversations; they are awful and, in my opinion, they are far worse for the poor HR person.

It transpires that unless you are explicit with the smelly one, they do not get it. Nine times out of ten a quick conversation will lead to great efforts for about two weeks, three if you are lucky. Sheila discovered this as within a fortnight of having THE CHAT with Dave, she had to again call him into her office. This time she had to explain to him that in addition to putting on clean clothes and undies everyday he needed to buy mouthwash, toothpaste and deodorant. Poor Sheila also had to stress that while in the shower he needed to wash every part of himself, including his man bits every day.

Morto. Most of us would buy a one-way ticket to Timbuktu. This however is often a part of life in tech companies where some developers and gamers barely sleep let alone do anything else.

It gets worse.

About a month after the second gory conversation Dave came into work and threw up all over the place, he was sick as a dog and could barely stand. Together with their colleague Andrew, Sheila managed to get him to the doctors who checked him over, diagnosed food poisoning and instructed him to get straight to bed. Sheila and Andrew knew that Dave had no family in town so they had to bring him home to bed. Nothing could prepare them for the sight of the bedsit they entered. It was filthy, rubbish had not been put out for weeks if ever. They tried not to look until they got to the bedroom, which was disgusting, there were no sheets on the bed just a stained duvet with plenty of stained magazines too.

Poor Dave, he made it into work a few days later and believe it or not was dismissed about six months later due to his poor hygiene.

Lessons learned

- When you have the smelly conversation, don't hold back if you are having the conversation for the second time. Afterall, everyone deserves a chance to rectify such smells, but only one chance. If it is a second conversation, make sure you use whatever language it needs to shock the person into meeting a bar of soap, remember they are not embarrassed by being stinky so it takes quite a lot to get through to them. Vague statements will not work. A manager I knew used a teddy bear and a pointer to point out the offending zones.
- Don't forget to rule out medical issues, if you have a company doctor, they can advise you. Although not common sometimes people have medical issues that might be at the route of the offending odours. A lot of

smaller companies don't have a formal company doctors' scheme but most GP practices will engage and help you with once off issues.

- Make your bed, you never know who will see it.

Common sense is like deodorant - the people who need it most never use it!..............

CHAPTER THIRTY
Cavities

Marie was tired, it was a long day as she had been in Brussels with her colleague Enda since the first "red eye" flight of the day. They had got along simply fine and she hadn't realised he was so nice and funny; he was relatively new in the organisation. After dinner in the hotel they retired as each had presentations to finalise for the next day.

Just before she went to bed Marie heard a knock on her door and looked out, there was Enda with his toothbrush claiming he had no toothpaste. Awkward or what! Marie made him wait and brought him out some and said goodnight again. Very uncomfortable at breakfast the next day Marie decided to be cool with Enda, she did not appreciate the late-night call.

The rest of the trip went ok but of course the minute Marie got back to the office she had to tell the story to the girls in her team who of course told their friends about Enda the new guy being a potential sex pest.

Before he knew it, Enda was called to HR for a friendly chat, friendly if you like insinuations that you are a sex pest. Enda burst out laughing during the meeting which did not go down too well. Enda pulled out his wallet and showed HR a picture of him and his boyfriend.

He did make up with Marie and they went on to become great friends outside of work, however you need to be careful when in situations like this.

So many people go crazy when away with work especially for the first few trips, they drink like mad, stay out till all hours and seem determined to treat the trip like their annual vacation. There is certainly nothing wrong with dinner and a beer but we have all been away with people who forget it is a work trip with meetings to be had, preferably not smelling like a brewery.

As often happens when groups go out drinking, things can get said, arguments can happen and before you know it someone takes offence.

On one trip I was on to Berlin years ago, I recall a senior project manager telling really disgusting racist jokes in front of the staff from Ireland who were with him on the trip. The same manager would have been very reserved and polite at home. There was hell to pay in the company on his return - two people made formal complaints that had to be investigated. The project manager of course had been too drunk to remember what he said and didn't say, and his staff were too nervous for their own jobs to tell the truth. The two employees who complained were then at war with the other two who would not corroborate their reports of that project manager. As a direct result of this single incident, this company banned all drinking on business trips.

Lessons learned

- ☺ Work colleagues are just that, so do not treat them like your BFFs.
- ☺ Leave early if an event is getting too rowdy and don't be apologetic about it.
- ☺ Always pack a mini toothpaste or a pack of mints or figure out where the nearest supermarket is.
- ☺ Never trust a woman not to share such a story with all her mates.
- ☺ Remember to never put yourself in a position where claims can be made or insinuated about you.

CHAPTER THIRTY-ONE
Call Out

Back in Fred Flintstone's time once you left work you really had no way of contacting colleagues until the next day in work. This is frighteningly recent. Mobile phones were not mainstream until I guess the mid 90's. So again, when researching for this book there were utterly shocking examples of people abusing mobile phones and text messages, here is an unbelievable list, all real

- A lady who had just texted work to say she had a miscarriage and needed a few days at home was asked to come into the office by her female manager for just an hour to finish payroll.
- An actual HR officer texted someone the day of their father's funeral to check where a HR file was left as it was needed in a hurry.
- A senior QA person told by text that if they didn't cut their two-week annual vacation short and return that they would have no future with the company.
- A supervisor who was disciplined for not answering email while on holidays.
- A senior management meeting held at nine am every Monday morning with issues to be discussed circulated on either Saturday or Sunday by the CEO, every week. No excuses for not being informed accepted.
- A junior manager refused a promotion because he had a policy of not answering emails after ten pm.
- A single mother of two who dropped the kids off every morning to school given an informal warning for not making alternative arrangements when texted at 7am to be in an hour early as a major customer was pulling their business.

- Staff being told at truly short notice to work Xmas Day despite having flights booked to travel to home which was overseas.

In all cases the staff felt terribly angry and annoyed at their treatment, which is counterintuitive as you want your staff engaged and motivated. Most staff these days check email at home and do not mind an odd interruption as long as there is give and take.

However, it does work both ways and many managers report employees abusing text messaging, some examples include:

- Texting in sick with vague details about their return and then switching the phone off so the manager cannot talk to them.
- Texting managers that you cannot meet a customer an hour or so before the meeting.
- Texting managers telling them that you are taking a day's holidays and bypassing the holiday approval process.

Lessons learned

- Set many boundaries in the staff handbook and staff contracts so that everyone knows what is expected from them.
- If you do look for extra effort occasionally then, make sure you reward in return.
- Move to a poor phone coverage / broadband area, best excuse ever.

CHAPTER THIRTY-TWO
Head Shot

Martina was thrilled, she had just secured twenty thousand Euro for a new facial recognition security system. The new security cameras would scan faces as people arrived to work and match to their photo on file. Bingo you are allowed access if your face is matched and no match will mean no access. Martina had spent a large amount of time getting permission from head office for this system and she really was diligent about the security of the staff and the company's property. The last thing she wanted as security officer was a break in or lapse in security.

There were 400 people in the company so it would be a busy few days getting everyone's photo taken and uploaded. How wrong she was!
There is now a generation who have grown up with an iPhone superglued to their palm, whose every movement and moment is photographed or recorded. This generation take their image profoundly seriously so there were ructions when it was suggested they would have their photos taken for the security system, the same security system bought to look after them and their jobs.

The company was a pharma company and staff were not allowed to wear make-up, jewellery or wear anything except their lab coats over their clothes. From the second the email was sent to supervisors arranging photographs to be taken of staff there was uproar. A strike was almost called! Philip one of the supervisors immediately had Catriona into his office, she was hysterical as no one, absolutely no one was going to take her photo without makeup. Regina was another example, she wanted to know what would happen to the image? Would it go on the company website? Did she have to do it? Karen, another employee came into her supervisor's office explaining that she was getting her hair highlighted the following Wednesday, the company would have to wait. Paul was the same. He was very concerned. He had started a new fitness regime and needed at least a month before he lost the last six kilos from his diet and his photo had to wait.

Despite it being made clear, this was a photo for a security system, the unrest continued, not with everyone but with a sizeable number.

It was decided that the company would allow the staff to take their own headshot and send it to Martina in security and give them two weeks to do so.
The results were hilarious. Martina said she still laughs when she thinks of the photos she received. Some of the girls were so made up that she did not recognise them. There were headshots, upper torso shots, a lot of cleavage shots, man without T-shirt shot, sultry shots, photos at least ten years out of date, photos with partners, photos at the Eiffel Tower, the list went on and on. Martina said the line-up of photos in the end was like Tinder with all the sexy poses people sent to work with no idea whatsoever that this may not be appropriate.

In the end a project that should have taken 3 days took nearly 3 months. Some of the photos were so out of date the brand spanking new computer system could not match the photo to the employee in question so new photos were requested.

Lessons learned

- Never ever underestimate how image conscious a generation who have grown up with mobile phones are.
- Think before you introduce new technology of any sort and how it will impact your workers.

- If your senior team is of a certain age, use a focus group to give feedback from different age groups. This works well and many companies use it when changing processes or making significant work changes. People are more likely to commit to a new process or workflow when they have been engaged in its design.
- Never put off getting your roots touched up, you never know when that important pic is needed.

Some interesting selfie facts,

- *According to Google, every third photo taken by those aged 18 to 24 is a selfie.*

- *Phones become best sellers based on the camera qualities that they have.*

- *55% of US plastic surgeons report seeing patients who want to look better in selfies.*

- *The percentage of male college students that share selfies on snapchat 50% v females 77%*

- *The average number of selfies that millennials are projected to take in their lifetime – 25,000*

- *According to the institute of advanced motorists – a shocking 9% of drivers admitted to taking a selfie while driving.*

- *The BBC reported in Oct 18 that 259 people between 2011 and 2017 killed themselves while attempting extreme selfies.*

CHAPTER THIRTY-THREE
Mickey Ds

Karl was the new software developer, he was brilliant at his job, he had started in the office and had hit the ground running. Karl was very quiet though, when having a sandwich in the office canteen he hardly ever spoke to anyone, most of the time he had his lunch at his desk or in his car.

His line manager was based abroad and the team was small, they rented an office in an exceptionally large building with many other start-ups. The building was confusing, a maze of corridors and offices.

One day another new hire started called Keith. Keith was much more outgoing and chatted to everyone around him, he had finished his induction on-line and was just about to start work when he asked Karl where the bathroom was? Karl did not know – he had been working for three weeks in the place and was using the next-door McDonald's bathroom.

Unbelievable but absolutely true, in time it emerged that Karl was on the Autism Spectrum, not that unusual in tech firms and not a big deal.

Karl's colleagues and remote manager were brilliant when it came to working with and managing Karl. They understood his need for structure and a quiet work environment and they helped him when he got stressed in work. This didn't happen often but occasionally when schedules got changed and deadlines got moved around Karl found that hard to adjust to. Karl was extremely happy in the role and after a couple of months interacted a huge amount with his friends and colleagues. It just took a few months for him to get to know people in work and for them to get to know him.

- Recognise that some people who are very introverted may be on the autism spectrum – make sure you are comfortable discussing with them anything you can do to help.
- Work with staff for solutions that meet their needs, many software developers work in absolute silence but some don't mind a busy environment.
- If you do have a staff member or more with Autism, go out of your way to get advice from your company doctor of from support organisations, they are both brilliant for helping and advising employers.
- Always, have a proper induction plan so quieter members of staff who may not ask too many questions are fully briefed and know who to contact if they have follow-up questions. A video induction is probably not enough, most people need the support of a colleague even if it is by phone or email.
- Locating near a fast-food outlet has many benefits.

CHAPTER THIRTY-FOUR
Work Related

Rachel was a tenacious salesperson; she had a team of five doing cold calling from her city centre office. Quarter after quarter she broke her own sales records. Selling subscriptions for her company's range of sports products was getting easier the more people became aware of the benefits of keeping fit.

Rachel turned over a lot of staff as she worked hard and played hard. Anyone who worked for her knew what was expected, head down and take no prisoners. As the company had a good sales bonus, staff knew they would be rewarded well. Over the years Rachel had parted ways with many staff who did not work out but to be fair to her Rachel did this generally within three months of the person starting. Rachel's reputation in the firm was tough but fair.

One Monday morning Rachel got introduced to Clodagh, Clodagh was the CEO's only daughter. Clodagh was twenty-nine, had jumped from one career to the next and stuck at nothing. Clodagh was a disaster, she stuck to the training at the beginning but soon there were days missed, loads of deadlines missed, endless personal calls to the office and endless excuses to take a long lunch. Clodagh was also lovely, a really nice chatty friendly person who made friends extremely easy but she had Daddy wrapped around her perfectly manicured finger.

Rachel had numerous meetings with Joe the CEO about Clodagh. These were very open and frank discussions but Joe always made excuses for her, "she was finding herself", "she had a tough break up", "she was missing her sister who emigrated"- endless excuses.

Rachel's team got very restless and at a team meeting told Rachel that she was blatantly favouring Clodagh. They never really considered that there was another side to the story. Rachel, fired up from the team meeting met with the CEO and told him it was Clodagh or her and guess what? Rachel was shown the door. A sad end to a brilliant sales career. Rachel, to be fair to her moved on very quickly to a bigger and better role and told me that without the run-in with her boss, that she would probably have clocked up another five years there without moving on and she was glad now to have moved.

However, there are loads of leaders out there, brilliant leaders who are totally blind to their darling offspring in the office. Luckily, Clodagh was lovely but I have heard of many little brats who are rude, brash and downright condescending to their colleagues just because their parents own or run the company (usually own it must be said)!

Lessons learned

- Think, think before you mix your work life and personal life.
- If your children are not getting on in other people's companies, they will not get on in yours.
- If you are running a family business and want your offspring to take over, make sure they build up their CV in other places first.
- Keep your offspring and animals away from the office.
- If you are suffering from a relation of the boss in your team and he or she won't get rid of them for non-performance then get out if you can. Do not waste your career working for someone who thinks so little of their staff that they allow them to be undermined like this. You would think in this day and age that owners no longer do this, think again, it is rampant. There is nothing wrong

with work experience or a summer job but I was really shocked to hear how many offspring are put into senior roles which at the end of the day does them no favours either.

"Treat your employees right, so they won't use your internet to search for a new job"
— **Mark Zuckerberg**

CHAPTER THIRTY-FIVE
Juggling Act

John was a really great software tester. He had worked for three years and was a huge contributor to the organisation, he had taken very little time off and worked many weekends. John was also very ambitious and had been promoted a lot throughout his career. One role he had not yet done was formal supervisory or management training. One September John decided he would enrol in a twelve-month night course to get a diploma in supervisory management, the problem was he needed every Friday off to attend classes.

John went to Becky in HR to discuss this and she was fully supportive of the course, in fact one of her sisters lectured in one of the subjects on it. Becky promised to talk to the CEO and get approval for the funding and time off. The company was lean enough and only supported further education on an ad hoc basis.

When Terry the CEO heard about the course, he went nuts! No way would he approve it. His problem was that it was too much time off for John and he was worried about deadlines being missed and productivity being slowed down.

That was semi true! What was really wrong with Terry was that he was a serial entrepreneur whose only goal was to sell the company, line his pockets and move on to his next challenge. Terry didn't care whatsoever about John's career trajectory or anyone else's. Terry instructed Becky to talk John into leaving the course for another year when work was quieter.

John was gutted, he lost interest in work and left within six weeks. He felt betrayed, he had given three years to help the company succeed but felt there was nothing in return.

- It is so difficult to work in a company when the owner or CEO has only one goal and that is to sell the company. Their motivation is to hit milestones and sell up.

- If you are in charge of HR and you really want to create a great company with a great culture, you will think very differently from your CEO. This is like walking on egg shells, you desperately may want to implement changes and policies that serve employees best in the long term but you are working for someone that is thinking very short term and is laser focused on an exit. In the example above John would have been so happy and committed if he had got to complete his course and his company would have benefitted, but the problem was that the benefits were in the future, a future that the CEO was not part of.

- CFOs have the same problems; they may want to introduce pension plans and medical insurance to protect staff and to help staff but the CEO will only see it as a cost.

- If you join a company and you are a HR person, my advice would be to try and figure out what the CEOs goals are. They may not be very open with you at interview stage but look at their bio and do your own homework. Remember too, if you clash with the CEO, your boss too often, your life will start to become miserable.

- Some multinationals are the exact same, they are just waiting to be acquired and the senior staff can cash in shares. They are often reluctant to think long term and that has huge implications for the people working for them.

CHAPTER THIRTY-SIX
Dress to Impress

Some of the funniest stories I have heard are around staff's clothes. With the general trend these days towards more relaxed clothing some people take this to extreme lengths and look like a hobo.
It's important for all team members to realise that not everyone appreciates the more extremes of fashion. For example, if customers or investors visit the office, they might not think that the office looks professional. Also remember if clothes are distracting, team members may be distracted. There are exceptions – such as video game development companies, but in general, business casual should not mean hobo, or indecent.

I spoke with a lady who used to work in IBM many years ago and after rearing her family went back to college and eventually re-joined the workplace. The change was shocking to her, back in IBM she had to wear tights, shoes with heels, skirts below the knee. On her first day back to work the HR executive met her wearing yoga pants and trainers with a skimpy T-shirt and her bra showing.

Some of my personal favourites clothing stories include:

- A website photo shoot planned from the waist up becoming head shots after a female executive turned up in a Dolly Parton cast off.
- Men in flip flops stinking out the office and going for lunch and putting bare feet up on chairs.
- Men and women going commando in see through trousers.
- Skirts so short they could be belts.

- A female HR manager sitting down with an employee and describing the pattern on her knickers as the girl didn't believe they could be seen.
- A girl who came back from a hen weekend wearing a F**K ME FRIDAY T-shirt, teamed with a pair of denim shorts and wore it into work.
- Men in sandals whose feet had not seen water or soap for a few weeks or months.
- Men in wife-beaters teamed with short shorts (think Neil Inbetweeners, Episode Thorpe Park).
- Clothes exposing all sorts of tattoos, one man with an "INSERT HERE" complete with arrow on his lower back. Another guy with a topless female tattoo on his arm.
- Thongs so high that they at least distract from the "tramp stamp".

Going back to the intro to this book, just think about how busy you are day to day in work. Then, think about the complaints starting about someone's shorts. Then someone else complains that their shorts are not too short! Then you decide to introduce a dress code - before you know it you have lost endless hours on what could have been sorted from day one.

Lessons learned

- If you are relaxed around dress remember your business may change and staff who were relaxed around the office may now need to go on site to customers or suppliers.
- Once a culture is established it is hard to relax it so start as you mean to carry on.
- You might think people have common sense and if meeting a customer might leave the pyjamas at home remember the old phrase, common sense is not that common.

CHAPTER THIRTY-SEVEN
It's a Wrap

Staff pranks are as old as the hills and some are funnier than others. One prank I do recall very vividly is when I was working in a software start-up. It was lunchtime and I was looking to see if anyone was around to grab a sandwich with. Upon entering the main staff office, I found one of the Chinese members of staff on the ground. I ran over to him and he was completely disorientated and speaking Chinese, even though he normally spoke perfect English in the office.

I thought he was after having a stroke or a heart attack, I kept asking him questions to see if he was ok but he kept answering in Chinese. I was distraught, I was screaming for help but no one was around. His chair was on the ground and he looked awful. I grabbed my mobile to ring for an ambulance when one of the other team members came in. I was so relived and started asking him to help me lift the person off the ground - however he burst out laughing.

Apparently, this person's friends and indeed the person himself, thought it would be very funny to spin him around repeatedly in his chair because he suffered from terrible motion sickness and then run off for lunch. When he had attempted to stand up however, he had fallen over and for whatever reason while dizzy and confused he thought he was answering me in English.

I calmed down eventually and was more than relieved that a colleague was not getting shipped to hospital.

Another prank I recall was in a Pharma company I worked in. A group of staff wrapped an employee who was leaving the company in bubble wrap and hung him off a high rack in the warehouse while they took photos and showed him off to everyone. In this case several members of staff were disciplined as damage was done to the storage racks costing tens of thousands of Euro. Thankfully, no one was hurt but they could easily have been!

I am sure these types of pranks go back as long as people are going out to work, however there is a big difference now.

1. With mobile footage, clips go viral and before you know it – millions of people could see your company and staff engaging in inappropriate behaviour.
2. An employee if injured - now has footage to sue the company.
3. If you are a Company Director, you could potentially get sued for breach of Health and Safety.

My own favourite story from the many I heard was from many years ago. There was a CEO who was a total "knob". He treated the women in the office appallingly. Every week he travelled through London Heathrow airport with just hand luggage for a day trip.

One lady who had worked with him for many years hated him as he was horribly disrespectful to her. A plan was hatched for her revenge. On her lunchbreak she went into Dunnes Stores (supermarket) and bought the biggest pair of "Bridget Jones Granny knickers" ever. Then she wrapped two knives from the cutlery drawer in the canteen in the knickers and when he was not around put it at the end of his briefcase (sooooo many HR issues around this particular action!)

No one was around to witness his next bag scan unfortunately but everyone had a great laugh thinking about him trying to find the knife in his bag.

These days you would probably be fingerprinted and arrested for such actions, and rightly so.

Managers can sometimes turn the tables and play tricks on employees, I recall years ago the CEO sent out a 40 page document on competitor analysis and somewhere on page 38 it read "If you have read this far, text me the word NOW and do not let your colleagues know you have done so". At our Monday operations meeting, he stood up and said how disappointed he was to have received no texts and then asked us to read page 38. All ten of us at the meeting had either not read or skim read the document and pretended we had read it. Very embarrassing all round but he thought it extremely funny.

The same manager called into his Financial Controller one day who had fallen asleep at his desk. The CEO took a photo, printed it, laminated it and hung it on his wall. Then he rang the Financial Controller to call into his office and waited to see how long before he spotted the photo! Brilliant!

Lessons learned

- Make sure you have a zero tolerance towards pranks in the workplace, no other lesson is needed here. Your insurance probably won't pay out on a claim and it is just a whole load of trouble that you just do not need.
- Never risk anyone's safety in the workplace. Over the years we have heard of accidents with falls and glue and staple guns, it is never worth it.
- Have google translate to hand if you don't speak Chinese.

CHAPTER THIRTY-EIGHT
Parcel Motel

When you work in a start-up, you work crazy hours and pre COVID-19, most of it was in the office. So, you need to be flexible with your rules as the team are giving so much of their time to help the start-up succeed.

Hello Amazon!

You will be amazed how many parcels can possibly arrive in a single office in a start-up. You will be stepping over them and they will be stacked everywhere. Tech staff in particular are forever buying books and gadgets. Throw into the mix shift workers who are not at home to sign for deliveries as they do not work normal hours and you really become a warehouse.

One manager Tom laughed as he told me that he was in reception when a large parcel arrived from "lovehoney.com", a sex toy site and not a site to buy bee produce. It was for a senior buyer, Seamus in the organisation so Tom was very discreet. Tom brought the package to his own office to store it awaiting a discreet moment to hand it over. The parcel though was very heavy and very noisy with clanging type sounds (no idea). Later that evening Tom was able to drag the parcel over to Seamus's office and he left it on the desk with a note explaining his discretion.

The next day Tom was at a meeting with six others in Seamus's office. The meeting was already in progress when he arrived and there on the floor, shamelessly was the lovehoney.com package. Seamus was no way bothered - not in the slightest. The meeting just went ahead as normal.

Tom never did find out what was in the box but was just dumbstruck at Seamus's brazenness.

Lessons learned

- Start as you mean to carry on - it is too risky to double up your office as a warehouse, all it would take is a trip and someone could be hurt and it would be very unlikely you would pass a health and safety audit.
- Keep your love life out of the office if at all possible.
- If you really want to keep a story discreet, do not tell someone who will publish it in a book.

Extract from the Daily Mail Newspaper

Several of Britain's biggest employers have reportedly banned staff from having parcels delivered to the workplace because their post rooms are struggling with the volume of online shopping orders.

HSBC, JP Morgan and Citi are among those who do not allow employees to have personal deliveries sent to their London offices.

The DVLA and the Department of Transportation also have similar policies in place.

Longer working hours and restricted delivery slots mean millions of Britons each year are choosing to have packages delivered to work - or face missing the postman.

CHAPTER THIRTY-NINE
Hole in One

No book on Irish workplaces is complete without mention of the US Visitors. There are almost a quarter of a million employed directly in US multinationals which represents a huge percentage of our overall workforce, circa ten percent. Add in the indirect suppliers to these companies and that number is significantly higher i.e. between 15% and 20% of our country reliant on multinationals.

The visit from the US CEO or senior personnel is like the in-laws coming to dinner on Xmas Day. The grass is cut, the building is painted, the car park is cleaned and the corridors are sterilised. There is no end to the efforts - I have seen machinery cleaning buildings, trees being planted, roads being laid, I kid you not. Having worked in five multinationals, I have seen this so often over the years that I indeed did it myself when I was a General Manager of the European Headquarters of a US Multinational.

Staff are briefed in advance so they know what is expected of them and the clever ones comply, the not so clever ones do not play the game! This is not cheating or putting on a false show, this is simply like dressing up yourself and your house for that dinner party you are hosting. After all, if you think about it, this is your only chance to really showcase in person what you are doing locally in Ireland. The best most successful GMs I know literally give up their lives for the week of the visit. They bring the visiting guests out to dinner every night and arrange visits to every possible tourist site in the locality and often further afield.

Note that if you visit the US, as the European GM you are seldom afforded anything similar in return, maybe lunch in a cheap diner but that is a whole other book!

One funny story I heard was from Andy a facilities manager at a US pharmaceutical multinational based in Ireland. The Friday before the big US visit there were over forty empty water bottles in reception - the five-gallon style ones. The receptionist was in a tizzy, the water people had not collected them as promised.

Andy was not going to let this ruin the visit so he loaded the drums up in his car. He did several runs back and forth to his house and stored the water bottles in his exceptionally large garage. This took him two hours but he was incredibly pleased that he may have "saved the day". The very next morning, which was a Saturday, Andy decided to go for a round of golf and opened the garage door to get his golf clubs. He forgot the water bottles were stacked in the garage and one of them fell on his head and he was knocked unconscious. A short while later his poor wife found him with blood all over his face. Andy was brought to hospital and had to wait until the Monday evening to be discharged after getting a CT scan. He returned to work on Tuesday with a massive cut on his forehead. He missed a day of the visit and he NEVER fessed up! He was way too embarrassed. He did end the water suppliers' contract though.

Lessons learned

- Make sure your team know why your company is doing all it does to win jobs and contracts, get their buy in, most employees are brilliant and help you all the way. There will always be the small few that don't see the bigger picture unfortunately and think you are crazy to go to such huge efforts to entertain visitors.
- Keep your golf clubs in your car.

CHAPTER FORTY
Park Life

This is a truly short chapter but I could not exclude it.

One Monday morning I started the day with a coffee with a visiting US CEO. He asked me what I had done over the weekend, I told him that I had visited Kennedy Park, a beautiful park in County Wexford outside New Ross built to remember President John F. Kennedy. Today it has one of the largest collection of trees from around the world staged in the most picturesque park one could possibly imagine. I would encourage anyone visiting Ireland to visit it and then take a short trip to New Ross and then Waterford City.

The CEO burst out laughing and said that it was the funniest thing he had ever heard as in his opinion -our entire country of Ireland is one big beautiful park.

I laughed it off but to this day when I am driving around Ireland and I look at our landscape - I often hear those words and feel utterly privileged to live in such a magnificent country.

Lessons learned

- Appreciate the beauty around you, especially if you live in Ireland.

Waterford Fact Sheet – if you are contemplating a visit or a new career.

- 30 Miles of Beaches
- Rivers & Lakes
- Mountains
- City Centre with Viking City Walls from the tenth century.
- 30 Mile Greenway, incredible walking/cycling trail along a former railway line, with a kids steam train for 5 miles
- Low Pollution
- Ireland's oldest City
- Amazing Institute of Technology with four Research Centres
- Motorway direct to Dublin
- Rosslare Port an hour away
- Cork airport 90 mins away
- Supportive Business organisations like Crystal Valley Tech, Waterford and Dungarvan Chambers of Commerce, Local Enterprise Office, Enterprise Ireland, IDA Ireland
- Strong IT, Pharma, Engineering and Science Sectors
- House prices and rentals less than half the rates of Dublin
- Abundance of great shared workspace like Boxworks and WorkLab with very reasonable rates
- A great tech meet-up scene pre COVID-19, much of which has gone online
- Multiple Museums
- Georgian architecture abundant
- Excellent Restaurants with exquisite locally sourced food
- Many food festivals
- Quality schools.
- A Gaeltacht (Irish Speaking Area)
- Waterford Walls, an annual amazing display of outdoor wall murals around the City
- Beautiful Golf Courses, Surfing School, abundance of quality sports clubs

CHAPTER FORTY-ONE
Open for Business

A year or so ago, I had the pleasure of being involved in a start-up boot camp. Teams were formed and each team had to pitch to a room of about one hundred people with their idea.

One of the first groups to speak, opened with a question "Raise your hand if you are seeing a counsellor or health professional in relation to mental health issues". I was shocked, I thought it momentarily outrageous that such a personal question would be asked in public.

What shocked me much more was the fact that roughly a quarter to a third of the people there raised their hands without so much as a flicker and continued to answer further questions about their start-ups.

The group were mainly 18 to 30-year olds and they were a brilliant group. They were full of innovative ideas and full of energy.

The workplace has changed, as attitudes to mental health have changed. There is still a long way to go but the willingness of a lot of young people to be open and transparent about their problems and needs is very encouraging.

Many of the larger companies I work with will often form focus groups or employee groups and give feedback to the senior team on how the workplace can be made happier and healthier. Many companies tell me that meditation classes and mindfulness classes at lunch time or after work are in huge demand nowadays. Some companies are paying for subscriptions to wellness apps and counsellor access for mental health issues.

If you browse the benefits that companies are listing in job adverts there is an abundance of benefits like gyms, employee wellness programs, flexi time, free snacks and fruit.

Only recently I heard of safe rooms, quiet calm rooms in companies that you can go to if you are feeling overwhelmed or need a small time out. Brilliant or what! For anyone who watches "Billions on Netflix", I seem to recall a safe room in the office which was used for many things that were not safe, like the prep for the boxing match or the "professional hugger"!

Many start-ups have been hugely successful servicing this new market that is opening up and genuinely helping people.

I personally believe that the next big trend in the wellness space will be to go beyond general stress management or wellness to "Vitality" i.e. helping the team not just cope with work and life but to actually thrive.

Thrive on the challenges that work and life presents every day, thrive on stress, thrive on deadlines, thrive on achieving work and personal goals, thrive on great social interactions, thrive on great spiritual insights and bring all of this together in an amazing sense of vitality or zest for life. Imagine if you could bring this vitality to your life and others. I believe this is the upcoming frontier of this space and I'd like to take this time to recommend the work of Dr Mark Rowe. He is the leader in "Vitality". Check out his website at the link below. Dr. Rowe is a Waterford doctor, author and TEDx speaker.

https://doctormarkrowe.com

- Do not shy away from talking about mental health issues with staff.
- Recognise that just because someone is going through a rough patch, it does not write them off forever, just like a broken limb, sometimes people just need some time to get through issues that are impacting them.
- Make sure you know how you can help staff.
- Even if you can't afford too many external supports you will find that many private health companies provide counselling and support and many GPs will work with you to figure out the best way to help your employee.
- Recognise that post COVID-19 we will all need to rethink how we support employees with mental health issues as the reassurance of face to face meetings may be a thing of the past.
- I believe the work being done in organisations on health and wellness is great, but it is in my opinion, just a start. I believe we are at the foothill of a mountain here and to reach the peak, and achieve peak personal and team performance, we need to go beyond "wellness" and move consciously and deliberately towards "vitality".

CHAPTER FORTY-TWO
Attention Deficit.

One of the most challenging things in organisations can be the expectation of many younger people and indeed some older ones to get things done fast - anything.

In an instant society where literally, everything is now available on demand, a whole generation exist that do not know how to wait for anything. They no longer watch TV-they binge watch, they do not have to think of a route - they google map it and they do not wait to buy books - they read them on-line etc.

So as a result, many team leaders report that it is proving extremely difficult to keep some people happy at work. In some professions there is a lengthy training in period and results are not seen for some time. I see this in software development. Some projects are multiyear implementations. Additionally, many software engineers join companies that they think are cutting edge, using up to the minute technology stacks and what they find is that they are maintaining and working around old legacy systems that will never be replaced. This can be hugely frustrating for some software developers. It is nearly impossible to do anything new and exciting and use all your talents when you must prevent the existing system from crashing. The task was described to me as trying to perform a surgery when the patient is bleeding all over the place. It can be very hard to plug the wounds and move on with the surgery simultaneously!

Add into the mix a short attention span and a desire to achieve things extremely fast and receive positive feedback e.g. "likes" or "thumbs up" just as quickly and this may not lead to positive outcomes for the company.

Sales, pre sales and cold calling see a huge turnover in staff, sometimes because the products are hard to sell but often because people lack the commitment and time needed to know the product, know the customer and learn the best way to sell it. The best salespeople take many years to learn their product and customers inside out.

Many HR managers I speak to tell me that they spend a lot of time trying to retain staff and keep them happy and that they acknowledge that often the employee will find the job boring and mundane but they just hope that staff will find other reasons to stick around. They report that it is getting extremely hard to keep young people on multiyear projects because the employee is not getting the instant gratification.

If you have staff who are bored, you are heading for trouble. Nothing is truer than the phrase – the devil makes work for idle hands.

If you have staff who are doing boring, repetitive tasks and they have time on their hands, many of them will have time to watch everything, they will have time to compare everything, they will have time to moan, to groan and to make life hell for HR. Not all of them of course, there will always be the majority who appreciate having a job, appreciate an income and will want to give one hundred percent in everything they do.

This is tough for managers, some jobs unfortunately are boring, some jobs require a lot of sitting around and doing very little and I am talking about all jobs, factory jobs, office jobs and some tech jobs.

HR can help team leaders in many ways to prevent boredom kicking in. They can help with upskilling and on the job training. If staff can continue to learn, to educate themselves and to have goals they are far less likely to watch everyone else and cause daily dramas over nothing.

Lessons learned

- Remember the old mantra, if you love what you do - you never work a day in your life. Hire people who love what they do and you will eliminate a lot of problems.
- Hire older people. People with a life's experience bring so much to an organisation. Make sure that when you focus on diversity that you also consider age a diversity issue and make a point of including those over 40 in your hiring plans.
- If you are stuck with staff who are struggling to stay committed to projects and or the organisation, give them side projects that they can own and work on in addition to their main job. This allows them to use more creativity and be happier. Usually the organisation benefits enormously too.
- Always encourage staff to upskill.
- If staff do have repetitive and boring tasks allow them to listen to music, the radio, headphones etc. as long as it is safe to do so. Some staff need to monitor cameras and screens etc. and it can be hard not to get bored, so do your best to help them.
- Match skillsets to jobs where possible, some people have great patience and can sit for long periods of time, other people cannot keep still for five minutes.
- Recognise that as you hire younger workers, they do have a different life experience so help them learn the skills needed to cut the mustard in your organisation.
- On a personal note I have to say that working with software people (developers, testers, designers etc.) is amazing as they are generally passionate about their work and careers.

CHAPTER FORTY-THREE
Text Alert

Texting has become an integral part of how many of us communicate. There are many texting mistakes that occur which are hilarious, some far too obscene to put down in print, some examples include the following:

- ❖ A girl who texted her boss after she had resigned informing him what would be her last day on the job but texted him her "lady day" would be the 15th of the following month. He was very confused!

- ❖ A new technician who texted her team leader a picture of a pair of spanx (or skims if you are American) and a thong along with a new dress asking which would work best? This message was meant for her sister Siobhan but she texted Simon her new boss. He referred the text to HR and on her third day in the company she had her first HR meeting. She didn't even realise what she had done until the HR manager showed her the picture of her own underwear. The mistake was quickly acknowledged and everyone laughed!

- ❖ Multiple examples of staff who are ranting about a colleague being "a dick", "a knob", "a bitch" etc. and then texting it to the person they are ranting about.

- ❖ A horrible manager who lost his phone, turned up at a meeting in an open plan office and asked one of the staff to ring his phone to see if it would ring, it did, but the employee who was ringing it had the manager's name in the phone as "Dog breath" and he forgot, so the minute he dialled the number called out by the boss who was standing over him - the name "Dog breath" appeared!

- ❖ A CFO who sent her entire organisation a group text starting Hi Gays, instead of Hi Guys.

❖ A new hire on her first day was talking to her new boss when her phone started ringing nonstop. Having no pockets, the phone was tucked in her bra. In the end the boss said, "can you just kill that please", she did, but not before fishing around in her bra first.

❖ An engineering manager Annie who was consoling her best friend the night before a meeting over the phone. The friend was distraught as the guy she had been texting for weeks had sent her some disgusting nude pics which she sent on to Annie to demonstrate what a dirt bag he was. The problem was the pics were now on Annie's camera roll! At the meeting, the next day with four men Annie was asked to show a photo of the new prototype motor she was working on. Annie took out her large screen mobile phone to pull up the photo of the new prototype and there they were, large as life, pictures of her friend's "man parts" – ouch!

Lessons learned

◉ If you do not have a separate work phone, think before you text.

◉ Be clear on your policies around the use of personal and work phones. I recall having to deal with a very upset lady who had been shown a very explicit image by her male colleague. The image was sent to him as a joke but he showed it to a group of colleagues. Most found it funny but it was a breach of company policy to share such images in their workplace.

◉ Sometimes you have just got to have a sense of humour when you screw up. It might be momentarily mortifying but it will pass.

CHAPTER FORTY-FOUR
Smile. You Just had a Big Night

So many men I meet think sexism is a thing of the past and that everyone is treated equally these days. OMG, if you think this, you have not a clue. While things have undoubtedly improved and they have – we still have a long way to go.

In my own career, twenty something years ago I recall one incident where I refused to do an asset audit in a shed where the facilities guys had "page 3 girls" hung all over their walls. I had a run in with the manager in question who would have been over double my age and asked me "was I intimidated because they were so sexy?". I in return asked him if he would have a problem if one of them was his daughter given that he had children that age. He reported me to my manager for being rude to him and I got reprimanded (but I never did the audit!).

I also recall being in a very large group of male engineers and being the only female present. The engineering manager asked where a certain engineer was and someone quipped "he is off breast feeding" aka he was on paternity leave and they all giggled like school children. I remember thinking back then, what a bunch of embarrassing children.

Even today when I answer the phone as CEO, so many men and sometimes women ask to speak to the CEO and when I say I am the CEO there is a minute's pause. As a sidebar, it is always interesting to hear the way people speak to you when they think you are the receptionist and you turn out to be the CEO.

I read a tweet only recently about a recently elected Irish politician who said her male colleagues were repeatedly complimented on their policies and she was told that she looked great!

When writing this book, I made it my business to talk to many twenty something years old females across pharma, IT and finance. So many still feel they have to work harder to prove themselves. Many feel they will not get promoted as they approach thirty as they are a risk for having children and they say it is really difficult at interview to secure a role if you are wearing a wedding ring and are late twenties early thirties.

On the flip side many men tell me they are frightened to say anything in the office, these days, in case they are misinterpreted and get into trouble! However, I think the solution to this is actually pretty simple – no to nude pictures, no to disparaging remarks about pregnancy, no to judging women by how they look and no to hitting on your female colleagues. Yes, to treating women just like everyone else, yes to taking women seriously and yes to holding women to account for their work. And for women – no to crying at the first sign of negative feedback.

For anyone who has watched the Hillary Clinton Netflix documentary - the scene where she is preparing for the presidential debate is very telling. The focus by her team is on her shoes! The men in the debates were no doubt busy swatting up on facts and figures but for Hillary, so much more was on trial.

Lessons learned

- If this is disheartening, just think at least things are improving and they are.
- Never partake in jokes about women, minorities, gay or older people etc. All of us can do our own bit to improve things.

- Always promote based on merit. However, given two people equally qualified for a job, one is male and one is female, I would always promote based on the needs of the team. For example, the more diverse a team is the more productive it is. The best innovation comes from a mixture of cultures, ages, sex etc. Quotas are a double-edged sword as no one wants to be the token woman or man occasionally.
- If you are in a senior position, know that you need to keep up with the pace of change and if you do not your company will suffer. Make it your business to be informed, to be willing to make changes and to ensure your workforce and management team are inclusive.
- If you are going to post a picture on social media of your senior team or board etc. and it is all "male, pale, stale and frail" be prepared for the backlash. It is happening every day of the week and I cannot help but think – "what were you thinking?", you would have to have your head under a rock not to realise that there is a new world out there and people expect and demand inclusion and diversity.
- I held a Tech Summit in 2018 and a young person asked me where the gender-neutral toilet was in the venue, I pointed to the bathrooms and said there is only male and female toilets, would the disabled toilet be ok? I got a tongue lashing that I still remember about how old and out of touch I was, how I was a disgrace to" hold a tech summit and not to have considered the bathrooms in the venue". It was an eye opener for me, it made me realise that a lot of young people feel very empowered and very confident standing up for inclusion.

CHAPTER FORTY-FIVE
Boston or Berlin

Evan worked in a US multinational; he was based in Ireland. The head office would often send across ridiculous memos trying to align work practices in the US and Ireland. For example, he recalled one where the US had decided that if two people were related, they could not work in the same company and had to decide among themselves which one would resign.

I kid you not.

Imagine trying to do this in Ireland, the unemployment register would soar and the other half of the workforce would go on strike!

There are so many examples I could list where HR leaders in multinationals thought they could behave abroad as if they were operating under the same employment laws:

❖ One HR executive in Canada thought that because she had worked in a European owned company in Canada that she was qualified to do HR in any country in Europe.
❖ I heard of a project manager in Ireland whose US based HR leader told her that she was to hire a new junior project manager. As there would be a lot of international travel involved in the new role, he told the Irish project manager that she was to hire a man for the role as they were easier to manage than women who "allowed their children to interfere with their work commitment". This was actually put in an email only a couple of years ago.
❖ A US HR leader who sacked an Irish software architect with no notice because he was becoming

very disruptive at meetings. No disciplinary meeting, no notice - he just sacked him and thought that was ok.

❖ A memo to an Irish General Manager over a weekend informing him to put an entire team on a zero-hour contract because the company revenues were falling off, to be effective immediately. There was no awareness of legislation in Ireland.

I am totally sure that Irish companies do the same with their foreign branches too i.e. forget the complexities of local legislation, I just do not get to hear about them!

Employment laws are different everywhere and when companies attempt to enforce policies that are illegal that is a major problem, for everyone involved.

For any company expanding into another country it is imperative that the right consultants or experts are drafted in. It may be costly to engage legal advice and consultants but without knowledge of the local employment legislation the company could end up in a lot of trouble with claims etc.

Lessons learned

- The best advice here is, "you don't know what you don't know", so pay for the best advice you can get.
- If you are taking up a role with a US company and they are new to Europe, make sure that they understand how completely different the employment laws are. This should not freak them out as they are completely manageable and good leadership locally will ensure compliance is kept.
- However, if you are an Irish Director and your foreign head office is asking you to implement processes that are not legal here, you could find yourself in serious trouble.

CHAPTER FORTY-SIX
Innovation Nation

Many companies are truly innovative and have great ideas. I remember reading that someone had registered the site easytoassemblemehole.com or something equally ridiculously brilliant for a business assembling flatpacked furniture.

Companies come up with genius products, some simple and some complex but both can be equally fabulous. Think about suitcases on wheels, I am old enough to remember lugging the heaviest of suitcases around the US in my twenties and now they are all on wheels. Simple but brilliant. Think about something really complex like "Ring Doorbells", enabling a person to monitor their home remotely and to talk to any person who is ringing their doorbell. "Ring Doorbells" can be installed in five minutes by simply connecting to the home's Wi-Fi.

This is reminiscent of a story I was told about a company who installed a "Ring Doorbell" at their company's front door for security. It transpired a short time after the doorbell installation that some of the younger male members of staff were spending most of their nightshift using the doorbell's video camera. They were listening in on staff from the neighbouring company who were having smoke breaks adjacent to the front door. They were also video recording "Ring Doorbell" footage from their mobile phones. One of the girls who was recorded discovered this as her cousin worked in the offending company (this is Ireland after all!)

But, back to innovation, some of the best HR leads I have worked with in recent years have come up with amazing ways, some simple ways and some truly innovative ways to attract talent to their companies. Here are some of the ideas that I thought were genius:

- ❖ Paid team lunches every Friday.
- ❖ Some companies pay the first three months rent for new hires, tax free and it helps the candidate if they are relocating.
- ❖ Many companies are not only giving shares and share options they are also giving an extra week's holidays to staff.
- ❖ Referral bonuses the equivalent of job agency fees paid out to staff who refers a new hire. If someone can make a bonus of Euro 10,000 for attracting a senior hire, they will make it their business to only bring in someone truly great. Contrast that with many recruiters who think far more short term i.e. take the fee and run!
- ❖ As much unpaid time off as a person wants. Think about that, most people can't afford to take loads of time off but many like the idea of it. People who can take time off are generally so appreciative that they work with the company to ensure it is planned and executed without impacting the company any way negatively. The flexibility that workers can now avail of is fantastic, once you keep it legal and the company can manage, you will find that workers are so appreciative of it that they will do a phenomenal job.
- ❖ Many companies have formed committees and focus groups that feed into the senior team on workplace improvements. Over time, workers get some of what they want and the company gets happy staff who stay.
- ❖ One large multinational that I worked for had an ideas box and you could literally put any suggestion forward anonymously, tell the CEO what she or he was doing wrong and the company worked religiously to tackle the issues.

- ❖ The paid for suggestion scheme is brilliant too, if you bring in a product / service improvement you get a large percentage of the first year's savings. I know many multinationals who have paid out tens of thousands of Euro and got multiples in return in terms of cost savings.
- ❖ Some companies now are doing the Xmas Party abroad and the staff pick the location, expensive yes, nightmare to manage, I can only guess yes. However, if staff don't leave your company, it might be worth it. Think of a senior hire paid one hundred thousand euro, if he or she leaves you, not only are you paying a recruiter but you then have a loss in continuity in the role and six months playing catch up.
- ❖ Four-day weeks and choose your own start and finish times. This gives incredible flexibility to workers, as long as it is workable with customer times etc.
- ❖ COVID-19 is and will continue to change the way we all work. Prior to the virus, a lot of companies did not like the idea of people working from home. This has now all changed and I do not think the world of work will ever be the same again.
- ❖ In Waterford in the local Institute of Technology, they are looking at the language used for advertising courses and it is helping them attract more females. See extract below from Time Magazine, April 2014.

Researchers from the Technische Universität München (TUM) showed 260 participants employment ads for management positions.
If the ads used words commonly associated with men, like "assertive", "independent", "aggressive" and "analytical," the women said they didn't find the job appealing and were less likely to apply. Conversely, if the job used words like "dedicated", "responsible", "conscientious" and "sociable"
they were much more likely to think the job was a good fit. Wording on the advertisements made no difference to men.

Lessons learned

- So how do HR foster innovation and ensure they have the edge on their competitors? This will be the challenge for HR over the next decade - we already have skills shortages globally in tech and engineering that are only getting worse. Like every skill, innovation can be learned, so get reading and upskilling if you are managing people or involved in a start-up company.
- Flat structures are far more innovative than hierarchical ones, let people think for themselves.
- Lead from the front, don't penalise efforts that fail and staff will be far more likely to be innovative.
- Female participation in tech, science and engineering has not improved much in recent years (worldwide and in

Ireland) and in some cases has declined. As a society we need to tackle this issue, from parents, to teachers, to leaders. We all have the future being defined by artificial intelligence, (AI). AI disruption of the economy will affect what jobs come and go over the next 5,10 and 20 years but sadly females are not playing a major part in defining this new world, in anything near the numbers that men are. This means that the innovation potential from 50% of the population is being largely lost. The same is true for many other minorities. Many tech companies are losing out on the advantages and successes that diverse teams bring. Having been immersed in the world of tech and tech shortages over many years I can see that there is no quick fix to the shortage of females in tech, what I can say is:
- Females are much more likely to have a tech career if encouraged by a parent or teacher.
- Females are more likely to be interested in tech if the career is positioned as caring or nurturing.
- Many females do not relate to a tech career because they do not really know what the roles entail unlike traditional roles which they do. Girls are often brought up to be more risk adverse that boys.

"Innovation distinguishes between a leader and a follower"
— Steve Jobs

CHAPTER FORTY-SEVEN
Back Tracking

Many of the founders and CEOs that I spoke to while writing this book have admitted to making huge mistakes, mistakes that haunt them to this day. They have learned from past mistakes and they all say the same thing - the sooner you own up to mistakes the better. Just like in life, you can't hide things and if you do, it will distract you from the rest of what you are trying to achieve. Mistakes they list included:

- ❖ Bad hires, believing what you are told at interview by a candidate versus how they actually perform in the role can often be black and white. Across the board the feedback was to do several interviews and not just one or two and always check references.
- ❖ Ignoring a worsening financial situation and constantly thinking that the next month will be better i.e. not facing up to the fact that cash is running out. Cash is king for a reason, if you don't have it or its equivalent nothing else you prioritise will matter. The number one priority should be survival.
- ❖ Acting unethically, e.g. selling a product that you know is not up to scratch, just to get some income to pay bills for example. I spoke to one founder who years ago was suffering financially and his wife was putting him under pressure to put down wooden floors in their home. Around the same time the founder was fitting out the company's office. The founder made the decision to charge all the wooden floors for his house to work. He was really the only person who knew this but he said he hated those floors at home and years later when they were replaced he said he actually felt a weight off his chest, it was his only dishonest action and it never sat well with him. There is a big difference between being

brave in work and taking chances versus outright fraud.

- ❖ A senior CFO I spoke to found it exceedingly difficult to work with friends and colleagues as she knew how bad the company finances really were. People would come into work having bought cars or taken out mortgages but she would be sick thinking about it. When she sought advice, she was told the same thing by friends and mentors. She was told "you have to keep quiet, if staff lose confidence in the company's future - that will be the nail in the coffin of the company" as people will leave. She did keep quiet, but later left to join a more established financially secure company where she said she slept a lot better at night. Her big mistake was moving to a start-up as it was not the right fit for her.
- ❖ Making deadline promises to head office, customers and suppliers that you know you can't keep.
- ❖ Constantly promising shares in the company or share options to key personnel but never delivering on it, then blaming the board, blaming the chairman etc.
- ❖ Selling companies and not looking after staff who may lose their jobs, particularly staff who have been loyal and brilliant along the way.
- ❖ Letting go staff due to pressure from head office when you have talked the same staff into leaving their permanent jobs to join your company.
- ❖ Pumping your own money into the business to the detriment of your own financial situation only for it to eventually fail.
- ❖ Being loose lipped on nights out, only for it to backfire on you.
- ❖ Not taking competitors seriously only to find yourself out of business.
- ❖ Not understanding consumer trends and getting it wrong – this is a big one, particularly in software!

❖ Designing software and not engaging with focus groups or experts first, assuming you know it is ok.

❖ Not knowing when to call it a day with a situation and when to ask for help. Many CEOs particularly on their first gig try to be all things to all people and are reluctant to ask for help. Women I think can be guilty of this in case it is seen as a sign of weakness.

❖ Not credit checking your customers and being burnt badly.

Lessons learned

☺ There are many lessons to learn in business and many of them the hard way but so many founders and leaders say the second time round after a failure is liberating. You will have been there before, that is if you have the will to do it all again. Interestingly people who build their houses say the same, that you never get it right first time. Some people say the same about their husbands!

☺ A surprising amount of the CEOs were honest with me saying that when they made their biggest mistakes, a little voice inside them was telling them something was wrong but they ignored it. They ignored the diminishing cash flows, the bills owed to suppliers that keep mounting, the CTO who was double jobbing and the list goes on. Trust your inner voice, believe in yourself and do not ignore it. One of the worst hires I ever made falls into this category. I ignored my inner gut feeling on the person but over time their true character emerged.

☺ Never try a cover up, think of Nick Leeson in the film "Rogue Trader". If you have not seen the film watch it. Covering things up will only make matters worse – "fess up and take the consequences". I read somewhere "What we fear most has already happened". On a flight out of the US some years ago the plane did several massive plunges in a thunderstorm and I developed a chronic fear of flying but I still had to fly for work. When I heard this phrase, it was like something clicked and I realised I was fearing the plane falling but guess what - it had fallen and I was still alive. I did an online course fearofflyinghelp.com and overnight got over my fear. I recall vividly my next flight which was a short hop to Iceland and I enjoyed every second of it, which was so liberating. So, face up to things, the outcome is seldom as bad as we think it will be. The longer you leave things in general the worse the outcome is.

- Having a supportive senior team is so important. I have worked for companies that truly worked together to solve problems and this was an incredibly supportive environment where everyone had everyone else's back. I have also worked in senior teams where there was fear, intimidation and backstabbing to beat the band. Guess what, no one wants to work like this and it comes down to the culture set at the very top.

- Help others - thanks to Crystal Valley Tech in Ireland, our group of founders have helped connect and create a strong network of people in the same sector - computing. This has proved truly invaluable and strong friendships have been formed from this work. There is now a network of people who genuinely want to help each other out. The benefits for both business and individuals have been enormous.

- Similarly, in Waterford, the local Chamber of Commerce run a Regional Leaders Program to develop leaders for the future. Participants get to meet one to one with existing leaders in the locality. This program has run for several years and has been hugely successful creating an incredible support network in the Southeast of Ireland. They also have some seriously successful people do group talks, where they are often open about their mistakes and misjudgements along the way. This is so reassuring to younger managers as it tells them "it is ok to screw up, we all did it and it will pass". A quote from Lynda Lawton sums it up

"The regional leaders' program has created a fast track route for young aspiring managers in Waterford and the Southeast, they learn fast, they learn from the best and they leave the program energised and ready to take on the world"

Lynda Lawton, Chief Operations Officer, Waterford Chamber of Commerce.

The Chamber must be doing something right as the Chamber of Commerce in Waterford dates to 1787 where the first minutes were recorded in Ireland's oldest City. This is quite incredible. Gerald Hurley as CEO continues to innovate to keep the Chamber very relevant.

CHAPTER FORTY-EIGHT
The Skills Gap

In a world where there is unprecedented growth in the need for IT, tech, pharma and engineering skills, there is an unprecedented challenge to companies. Should they accept second best and hire an average or below average candidate or hold tight until they get the dream candidate?

This is a tricky one and I among others have been burnt by bad decisions here. Let us explore the options,

❖ Option 1- You might hire a person in a hurry just to fill the slot as you have so much pressure on you to find someone. This might entail going against your gut feel that the person is not the right person for your company or for the job. So why would you do it? There are multiple reasons why you might do it. If you are a multinational, you risk the job going to a different country if you cannot fill the role or you might risk the wrath of the angry CEO if you cannot fill the role. So, you might give in and take a second-rate candidate and cross your fingers. Some of these people grow into what you hoped they would be, others just do an average job. The worst case - you get someone below average who just never makes the grade. In the latter case, you may be facing into some serious HR issues managing a poor performer and you only have yourself to blame. Jill told me once where she advised a CTO not to hire a candidate who at interview smelt of alcohol. His CV was excellent, his experience was second to none but he had a slightly shaky hand and had barely masked the smell of a late night. He got the job, he did a great job, when he bothered to turn up and eventually got fired.

❖ Option 2 - You do not fill the slot as you hold out for that perfect candidate. You might strike it lucky or you might not. You might wait so long that you lose your competitive edge, you might risk your own position if you are in HR as you may be measured on number of new hires. This too is a gamble just like the example above of taking the wrong person. I spoke to Louise who worked for a general manager who would not compromise, he absolutely wanted to wait for the perfect candidates to come along for two key positions. When head office in the US got frustrated Louise's, boss threw her under the bus and she eventually lost her job for poor performance.

❖ Option 3 - The ideal situation is that you have a roadmap in your company, you know the hires you will need so you start several years in advance. Lots of finance, engineering, pharma and tech companies are doing this. They are cultivating relationships with schools and colleges. They are getting their brand out there and they are working hard to ensure a pipeline of candidates to their company. This is very laudable but it takes time, it takes money and it takes great vision. Some companies have one out of three of those attributes but very few have all three. If you are a start-up company it can be hard to think years in advance as your focus will be on hitting your metrics to get to your next investment round. Also, if you haven't got a dedicated HR person, you are probably not even thinking past the next customer trial, the next product release let alone three years into the future.

Lessons learned

◉ It takes a village - skills gaps need to be identified by governments and they need to work with industry, education and research institutes to find ways to tackle skills shortages and to try and ensure that they are resolved. One great example in Ireland is the springboard program which is a program to accelerate the obtainment of third level honours degree which would normally take four years. Springboard courses take only two years. Wow, what a game changer this is. Similarly grant aided/subsidised apprenticeships are a great way to fill gaps and give great careers to a whole generation. In Ireland unlike many other countries, we have been far too snobbish about the apprenticeship route. Some of the best employers have themselves come through the apprentice route and they know their trade inside out and upside down. They are also passionate about their sectors and have great houses if they are builders, plumbers etc.

- Parents and career guidance counsellors need to be thinking of careers in a different way. In a society that will see more roles than ever be replaced by automation, their role as advisors is more crucial than ever.
- CEOs and HR leads need to make it their business to network. They need to know the courses and supports available to their sector both locally and online. Cluster organisations like Crystal Valley Tech or Chambers of Commerce are phenomenal vehicles for getting to know your peers and for having a network of people that you can pick up the phone to for advice.
- The costs of upskilling can be substantially reduced if done in numbers. Get some like-minded companies together and speak to your local college about ensuring the right courses are on offer. In fairness the colleges are incredible nowadays for engaging with industry and identifying skills needs.

CHAPTER FORTY-NINE
Departures

Some incredibly sad stories from organisations emerge from time to time. With the international movement of people, it often occurs that an employee may live in your country but not have a single relative there or indeed any close friends.

I have heard of HR staff and CEOs having to arrange funerals for people who literally do not have anyone in the world to bury them. I have heard of staff becoming terminally ill and the local management having to track down relatives and inform them, often when English isn't their first language. In one harrowing case, an employee was tragically killed in a car accident and the relatives abroad had to be informed by his employer.

Obviously, the death of a staff member who is from your own country is terrible but at least their loved ones are around to make arrangements. It is just the saddest thing to hear of someone dying alone in a country.

Lessons learned

- There are many lessons to be learned. Always have up to date contact details for staff and their next of kin, you sadly never know when something might happen.
- No matter what happens, reach out immediately and sympathise with the person's family.
- Have proper life assurance in place. At least this way the person's family or nominated individual will get a financial pay out. This may sound crass but if a person has to be repatriated home and buried, the cost to the family may be enormous. Every single CFO and HR manager I believe has a duty to have a life assurance

policy in place. They are not expensive in the scheme of company costs. They also have a duty to inform the relatives of the deceased immediately about the life assurance. At least this way the family who might have to borrow for a funeral will know some funds are coming. Awful as it is, bills have to be managed and paid.

- Arrange counselling or grief therapy for staff who may have been impacted. There are great services out there and your staff may need help to cope with the loss of a colleague, particularly young people who may not have been through something like this before.

- Reach out to ex-employees who worked with the deceased individual. They will have had a relationship with the person and might like to be informed or given a chance to partake in a service or memorial event.

- Do not put any details on social media, on emails and be incredibly careful about the communication around sensitive issues like death. I personally recall working in a company years ago where a man committed suicide. It was horrific but I always remember a young member of staff coming into work and telling everyone about it in explicit detail. This was a time when suicide was not spoken of and it was terrifying to people in the office and very disrespectful of the person's memory. There was also a question mark back in those days if life assurance would be paid out if suicide was the reason for the person's death.

- If possible, do something in your company to remember the person on their anniversary.

CHAPTER FIFTY
Begrudgery

I recall an engineer Gavin who worked for me. His wife had some difficulties with the birth of their fourth child. For a while it was questionable if the baby would be ok which thankfully, he was.

A colleague at the time actually said to me that he was secretly delighted that Gavin's birth plan had not gone smoothy. I was shocked and sickened. How could anyone speak like this about a new baby and mother? It disturbed me in a way that no other single comment in my career has done so. When I told him that his comment was disgusting, he backed down a bit, claiming that Gavin was very blasé about the time off he would need etc. Undoubtedly the most psychopathic behaviour I ever experienced from a colleague, and believe me when I say, if you have worked for CEOs you will have many awful comments to choose from!

This single experience showed me that some people are just jealous and nasty and begrudging of other's successes and achievements. A truly horrible trait in a person.

Social media I believe can be somewhat to blame for jealousy and feelings of inadequacy. Instagram shots as we all know portray that perfect life, perfect wife, perfect family, house, career etc. Social media does not show the work and sacrifices that people have made to achieve success.
However, if the successful person is showcasing their wealth on social media – it is hard to have sympathy when they are trolled!

- Make sure in your company that you create a culture that celebrates other people's achievements and a culture that is positive and happy. Make no room for begrudgery.
- The overwhelming majority of people I have met and gotten to know are really good people.

"You will never reach your destination if you stop and throw stones at every dog that barks"

— **Winston Churchill**

CHAPTER FIFTY-ONE
ADVICE FROM SOME FOUNDERS & CEOS

When I finished this book, I went back to my Board of Directors and I asked them to give me advice for HR managers and employees, both who might be at the start of their careers. Here is the top ten of each. If you learn something from it - great.

ADVICE TO HR PROFESSIONALS

♥ 1. Do not be side-lined

Too many leaders of tech organisations see finance and HR as secondary to technical skills. Nothing is further from the truth; no company will succeed without all parts of the organisation contributing. Fight your corner if you are the HR lead to be at the senior table, do not get "fobbed off" and report to one of the other managers.

♥ 2. Culture every time

Be a driver for change in your organisation. Buy into the culture of the company you are joining or be part of the design of the culture in the company you are founding. Continue to cultivate an amazing work culture, this will not only make your organisation a fantastic place to work, it will also reduce the issues you have to deal with as busy happy employees do not have too many HR issues. Having worked in five multinationals the one common thread I see more than anything else is that the successful ones truly work to the same goals and bring everyone along with them. One of them even had the value of "Disagree and Commit", get it off your chest, voice your opposition but at the end of the day you support the team decision and work together.

♥ **3. Value older people**

In our ageist society, the most experienced people struggle to get employment, yet they are the staff who will work the hardest, cause you the least amount of issues and often bring the best ideas to the table.

♥ **4. The 99% rule**

Give 99% of your time to the 99% of staff who are good, honest, work hard and support the team and the company's mission. Too often the 99% of HR time is given to sorting out the bad 1%. Do not let bad individuals monopolise you and know when to call it a day. If there is a bad egg, you will not win. Pay what you need to pay and go your separate ways. This will seldom happen and most people will be able to work with you to resolve issues that do come up.

♥ **5. Be a legal Eagle**

Know your HR legislation inside out so that you don't get tripped up. A lot of HR is sorting out situations that should never have happened. Have HR support from employers' organisations. Join groups of HR professionals and have a likeminded group to support you.

♥ 6. Use HR Software

Get the best software to suit your company and use it to the best of its and your ability. Having information that is accurate and at your fingertips is invaluable. If you inherit an old system, have your plan in place to ultimately replace it.

♥ 7. The CEO not the staff should be your best friend.

Just like the CFO, you need to be inside your CEO's head, you need to know how he or she thinks, you need to know everything that is going on. Too many entrepreneurial founders go it alone only telling finance and HR after the event what they have done. This is not good enough and not the right thing for investors or staff. This is not to say you can't debate and argue positions out from time to time but to really work together you need to have the same vision and goals and agree the best way to execute them.

♥ 8. Versatility

You cannot beat HR people who have moved around and know organisations from many angles other than HR. This means they understand corporations very well. So, don't look at a varied CV as someone who doesn't know what they want, view it as someone who has vast experience to bring to the table.

♥ 9. International Presence

If you are working in HR and your company expands into other countries, understand that "you don't know what you don't know". Get a local person on the ground, an employee, a consultant or somebody who can advise you. Too often we see US companies thinking they can run HR from the US, which often results in mistakes, there absolutely needs to be someone on the ground.

♥ 10. Happy Employees seldom leave

Another old phrase which is absolutely true, people generally stay in companies if they are happy there. It is NOT your job in HR to keep staff happy, rather it is the job of the entire senior team that you are part of but you can be a driver and an innovator in this area.

ADVICE TO EMPLOYEES

♥ <u>**1. Keep Learning**</u>

This advice is the one that everyone is advocating, as computers continue to replace jobs in many areas, the skilled will survive. No matter what role you are in, no matter what age you are, keep learning. There are so many resources now with Coursera, Edx or other online course websites. Most Coursera courses are free if you take the "audit the course" option. There are also many other free resources online in addition eBooks and audio books. Keep adding to your skills and Girls - the less time you spend on the "Daily Mail" website the more time you might learn something useful on another site – note I am sometimes guilty of this one. Being able to list out all Kardashians in age order is not a life skill.

♥ <u>**2. Be Versatile**</u>

People who have clocked up careers in different disciplines, no matter what they are, learn loads, think differently and make great employees. Take every chance you can to step outside your comfort zone and keep adding to your abilities. The days are gone more or less when one career did you for life, nowadays it is all about reinventing yourself. We see journalists constantly reinventing themselves as print media declines and we see traditional supervisors upskilling as automation replaces many roles in manufacturing.

♥ **3. Be Resilient**

Grit and Resilience will see you through life and through a great career. Make it your business to read about resilience and if you are lacking in it, start cultivating it. The best employees who thrive in their careers are the most resilient ones. Never believe anyone who says you cannot change your makeup. Everyone can change – google "neuroplasticity" if you don't believe me. If you aren't born resilient you can't change it – you can and you should. Interesting research shows how children from challenging backgrounds can be the most resilient because they must be. Software engineers are incredibly resilient, the feedback they give each other at scrums can be brutal but they suck it up and become even more brilliant.

♥ **4. Don't make enemies**

So much of business is networking. Do not burn bridges. As much as you may want to tell your manager when you resign that he is a "merchant banker", hold back as it may hurt you in the long run. Ireland is small but so is the world. You never know when you might need someone. Most people can very quickly check up on you due to the few degrees of separation that we all have.

5. Work hard

"There are no traffic jams on the extra mile". I love that expression because it is so true. Any of the seriously successful people I have met have worked like "dogs" to get there. I see some a new trend for some people to use countdown apps to five pm and I admire their discipline and order but I wonder how they will make that leap to big success, if that is what they want. Elon Musk apparently said that "no one changes the world working a forty-hour week". Life is a trade-off and I have yet to meet someone, anyone who has it all. More time in the office is less time not at the office and vice versa. Big careers are not for everyone and if you want to have a great work life balance, go for it, but don't expect to have it all. But don't begrudge anyone else's success.

♥ 6. Set Goals

There is absolutely nothing new in this but without direction you will have no direction. Realise that you are much more likely to reach goals if you set them. Drifters drift and goal setters reach most or some of their goals which is better than not having any in the first place.

♥ 7. Take Responsibility for your actions

Do not be a "whinge bag". No one will want to be around you and no one will want to work with you. Whingers are draining, the sort of person who blames everyone else for everything. We are all busy people and in general do not want to spend time with people who do nothing but moan, whine and blame others. Particularly hard to spend time with are those that blame others for their own failings, mistakes or lack of progression in life. If you make mistakes, own it, if you screw up – admit it. Acknowledge the mistake, learn from it and do better next time.

♥ **8. Do not crave praise**

Do a job and seek constructive and honest feedback. Always try to improve. If you become like the Facebook or Instagram junkie who is only interested in likes, over time your team lead or manager will not give you the type of honest feedback required for your growth. With so much time spent online and so much brain pleasure achieved from those little likes, there are many managers that have told me that they see more and more people that recoil from any constructive feedback. But this does you a disservice as this type of feedback is required for growth by everybody.

♥ **9. Have Mentors**

No matter how old or how successful you are, always have a person or people who will help you - people you can learn from or people who will hold you accountable for your "BS". Not only does this keep you humble but it drives you forward. In my role running a Tech Cluster – Crystal Valley Tech, I speak to CEOs and leaders all the time and I am always struck by how they want to learn from others all the time.

♥   **10. Love what you do**

As Confucius said, "Choose a job you love, and you
will never have to work a day in your life." So, it
sounds like a cliché but do what you love. Or another
way of looking at this is to seek out the meaning in
your work. For example, how do you contribute to
yours and others lives through your work? There is
another great saying, "What is for you won't pass you
by". If you cannot make a living out of what you do,
still do it as a hobby. Loads of CEOs and founders
despite their crazy workloads and long hours find
time to volunteer on residents' committees, GAA,
youth organisations and the list goes on. They are
always the ones who will sit on voluntary boards,
give time to help others and rarely say no.

FINAL REMARKS

Whatever the future holds, people and companies are incredible flexible and we will all find our way and we are in the enviable position of influencing and being part of the new normal.

♥ 1. Managing Productivity

While most people will embrace working from home, there will be the small minority who abuse the trust needed to make it work. This is already a challenge for companies and will continue to be so.

Many leaders are old school and do not like the idea of working from home for a multitude of reasons, a lot of which boils down to lack of trust in their people. They are going to really struggle in a post COVID-19 world.

The solution to this is to get out of the mindset of the micro manager or controller. Focus on output measures such as objectives and key results (OKRs), then build reward systems around outputs.

♥ 2. Loss in Team Momentum

When you meet virtually, it is never the same as meeting in person, you don't get to read the body language of your colleagues and you don't get to chat with them before and after the meeting where sometimes the best ideas are generated. There is also great bonding from staff lunches and events and travelling places together.

Meeting virtually is not as relaxing; most people do not want to be staring at screens for endless hours.

With the cutbacks in business travel, I think women have an opportunity to compete on the same level as men. Too often senior executives are men, and women are in the minority and the social events arranged on business trips tend to be more masculine like watching a match, playing golf with clients etc. With men not having the edge by getting to have more personal relationships with clients, customers and overseas colleagues, women can compete on the same level.

♥ 3. Workspace

Not everybody has room at home for a proper office, not everyone has good broadband. There will continue to be a growth in hot desks and shared workspaces but it presents a real challenge to employers. They need to ensure their staff have the proper tools to do their jobs well.

What if one of your best employees moves to a new house and the Wi-Fi / broadband is substandard? What if there are power outages and no backup generators? What if children are noisy / at home sick?

♥ 4. Security

As more work will be done online there will be more hackers and security breaches. This will be a big challenge for companies to manage. Even statutory requirements to keep hardcopy documents becomes harder and poses more security issues in a post COVID-19 world.

♥ 5. Managing health issues and personal disruptions

Mental health issues and issues like bereavement, divorce, family issues are much easier to manage and help with in person than at a distance. The isolation for many people will only exacerbate issues and coping. The reassurance of speaking face to face with an understanding colleague or manager will no longer be there.

♥ 6. Culture

Culture can be hard enough to proliferate in a physical workspace. How will management do this in a working from home culture? It will be harder, but it can be done. This is so important as the success of many organisations is down to their incredible cultures.

♥ **7. Performance Management**

Many managers are extremely poor at managing performance and now more than ever it is going to be imperative that employees have objectives that are measurable and reviewed regularly. If management fail at this task there is a huge risk that the employees will lack direction, will take the wrong direction and will not be successful.

♥ **8. Processes**

The documenting and following of processes will be more important than ever in a post COVID-19 world. Individuals and teams will need to be crystal clear about how and when they fit into the company processes. There will need to be a huge back office effort to support staff, and who will support the back office?

♥ **9. The Water Cooler chat**

How will employees find out the latest gossip, hear the latest rumours, laugh at the gaffs they made at the earlier meeting?

Where will the fun be in the new world of working from home? So much of the post COVID-19 world is not defined. There is no rule book. We will all have to figure it out. Right now (October 2020) as I write, we are still waiting for post COVID-19 to arrive, so until then it is all speculation.

♥ <u>10. Romance / Leg over</u>

With so many people meeting their partners at work. How will people meet people? I think dating apps will explode. Think about it, depending on what survey you read, between 20 and 50% of people meet their partners at work. Working from home will leave a big gap to be filled!

So many of the HR issues in this book could have been avoided by better communication, at induction, at performance reviews etc.

In a post COVID-19 world we are probably going to communicate in a variety of ways, far more than in the past.

We need to be able to write clear emails, communicate effectively on video calls and be concise on phone calls. If there is one skill that will help us thrive in the new world, it will be our ability to communicate very clearly.

"The way we communicate with others and with ourselves ultimately determines the quality of our lives".
Anthony Robbins

Printed in Great Britain
by Amazon

54886380R00080